The male makes every effort...

...but the female shows no interest.

Getting to Know Each Other

If both partners are still very young, it may take several months before they become a true pair. Fortunately, the forces of nature are strong.

Brief resignation on the part of the male...

There are some very shy cocks that don't dare take the initiative or do so only reluctantly. Then it is often the hen that lets the male know what she expects of him in terms of courting and mating.

...followed by a renewed attempt, this time more urgent.

i

A little coyness is in order at first.

Finally, she turns to him with a loving air.

Now the hen even lets her partner feed her.

Courtship Begins

During the mutual wooing and in the courtship displays the same situations recur repeatedly. Sexual excitement is sometimes expressed passionately and sometimes takes on an air of gentle devotion. The male is most impressive with his courtship displays, whereas the female seems rather passive.

The Parakeets Mate

The important thing now is to maintain the balance...

It is touching to watch a parakeet female settle down to mate after her apparent initial disinterest. She "lies" down on a branch almost horizontally and raises her tail up, looking at the male the whole time. The latter overcomes his inborn shyness for a moment and climbs onto her back. Most cocks wrap just one wing around their mate, but some use both wings. Then the birds press their vents together so that the semen penetrates to the hen's oviduct. However, not every mating works smoothly. With young birds it often takes some practice before they are able to transfer the sperm successfully. Feathers around the vent that are too long can also interfere with fertilization. It is important to supply cage birds with stable natural branches on which they can get a good hold for mating.

...so that copulation can be accomplished successfully.

After all this loving, rest is good.

Parakeets are excellent flyers. If they are kept in cages, they need plenty of free flying time.

What is the difference between birds and other vertebrates? Actually, only the feathers, which allow birds to fly. A bird's entire organism is adapted to life in the air. Even though parakeets feed on the ground and sleep in the tops of trees, they wouldn't survive if they couldn't fly.

The Author
Annette Wolter is a bird expert with many years of experience in parakeet care, and the author of one of the most popular books on parakeets. Her ongoing contact with veterinarians, ethologists, and breeders enables her to keep abreast of current avicultural developments.

The Photographer
Monika Wegler is a professional photographer, a journalist, and author of books on animals. She specializes in animal portraiture and in studies of dog, cat, and parakeet behavior.

Special Advisors
Klaus Stark, practicing veterinarian, for the chapter *If Your Bird Gets Sick* and *Glossary*. Herbert Hummel, chairperson of the Association of German Standard Parakeet Breeders, for the chapters *Parakeet Offspring* and *Breeding Parakeets*.

Annette Wolter
Monika Wegler

The Complete Book of
Parakeet Care

Expert advice on proper management
160 fascinating color photos
Tips on parakeet care for children

Consulting Editor–Matthew M. Vriends, Ph.D.

BARRON'S

CONTENTS

Preface

Everybody loves parakeets, but do we know what it takes to make this small parrot from Australia comfortable with us?

The *How-to* pages contain the author's advice on choosing the right cage, building a bird tree and a hanging perch, providing first aid, and tips on breeding and rearing parakeets.

On the *Question* pages the queries most often asked by parakeet owners are answered. These questions are based on the many letters the author receives from readers.

The *Tips for Children* include important rules young parakeet owners should observe, suggestions for toys children can make for their parakeet, and an account of parakeet life narrated by the bird.

The *Glossary* includes all kinds of interesting information concerning parakeets along with explanations of some more technical terms.

The photos are all exclusive new pictures. They convey in vivid form what these little birds "are all about."

This new Barron's pet owner's guide is designed for everyone who likes parakeets and would like to learn more about them.

The author and the editors of *Barron's Nature Series* wish you good luck with your parakeet.

My Friends, the Parakeets

Over the years I have come to love these small, lively birds more and more. I have not only owned a number of parakeets myself, but have also gotten to know many that belonged to other people. I have, in fact, published several books about these fascinating members of the parrot family, and through my active correspondence with other parakeet owners, I keep hearing new and remarkable stories. However, there is one thing that has become clear to me, both from my own personal experience and from my reading about parakeets: Love alone is not enough to create a healthy environment for these birds.

Keeping parakeets properly is not easy. This becomes particularly clear if one considers how these birds live in their natural habitat in Australia. The first chapter of this book describes the life of wild parakeets. The birds are used to living closely together in large groups. Their entire day is taken up with activities essential for survival. Food has to be gathered and nesting sites found. Potential enemies may lurk anywhere, and constant watchfulness is therefore required. A parakeet living under human care is relieved of all these "worries," but the original patterns of behavior are still "in the blood," even of birds that have been bred in captivity for decades. That is why pet parakeets must be kept busy and, especially if they are kept singly, require a lot of love and attention from their human surrogate partners. So, be sure to devote as much time as possible to your bird! It will respond with affectionate trust and enrich your life with its varied repertoire of behavior.

Remember that parakeets are meant by nature to live in large flocks and that one that is kept singly will inevitably suffer from loneliness. No matter how hard you try, you will not be able to really replace an avian partner. I therefore advise all prospective parakeet owners to acquire a second bird. Parakeets display their full range of vocal communication and body language only in the company of another member of their species.

Keeping parakeets means taking on a responsibility. Birds are not inanimate objects that can be put aside when we tire of them. They need constant love. And you will have to provide them with living conditions that meet their natural needs, at least partially. Thus, it is very important that the birds spend some time every day outside the cage. In the wild, parakeets do a lot of flying, and they should be able to fly freely when they are kept in homes, too, to keep them from becoming fat and lazy. They should also have opportunities for climbing, such as a bird tree offers, to provide needed exercise. Don't forget that an apartment harbors many potential dangers for birds. Make sure no hot stove burners are exposed or containers full of water left uncovered. They could spell disaster. You'll be compensated a thousandfold for the trouble you take and the inconveniences you put up with by the lively activities of your birds. I never tire, for example, of watching my birds investigate any object within their reach to explore its potential for play or to chew on. They display an amazing inventiveness at finding new uses for all sorts of items. Any small cavity is examined to see if it could be used as a nest; a ballpoint pen held by a human hand becomes a balancing beam; no crack is too narrow to try to wriggle through. Discomfort and protest are expressed as openly as sadness, love, and exuberance. Sometimes the birds get carried away with excitement and pinch "their" human hard enough to hurt. There's no ill will in this; the birds simply don't realize that humans lack a protective layer of feathers.

If you decide that parakeets are the right birds for you, you will find that you have chosen a potential treasure that will reveal its full beauty if you provide the proper conditions and care along with love and attention. I wish you many happy and fascinating hours with your parakeets.

Annette Wolter

This bunch of spray millet would be more than enough for several birds. For only one parakeet, it is too much.

It would be wonderful to have a partner to scratch one's head. However, this bird has to make do with a stiff string.

At Home in Australia

We all know what parakeets look like because they are one of the most popular cage birds in the world. But where did this lovable and lively small parrot originally come from?

Wild parakeets are found only in central Australia, where they live under harsh conditions—hot days and cold nights, long periods of drought, scarce water, and scant food supplies. The birds crisscross their vast range like nomads, searching for food and water.

A number of scientists have studied Australian parakeets and described their life in large flocks, smaller groups, and families. Knowing how parakeets live in nature can help us create relatively favorable conditions for our pet birds and avoid mistakes that would violate their nature.

"Budgies"

The Australian aborigines called these small parakeets "betcherrygah," which means "good bird" (good also in the sense of good to eat) and suggests that their diet included these birds. Around 1840, when the English ornithologist John Gould brought back the first live parakeets from an expedition into central Australia, the English called them "budgerigars"—an anglicization of the Australian name—from which "budgie" is in turn derived. In America, the official name of the birds is Australian shell parakeet, which is usually shortenend to just "parakeet." All wild parakeets have yellow heads, are green on the back and underside, and have a pattern of parallel wavy lines on the back of the head. Their scientific name is *Melopsittacus undulatus Shaw*. The Latin means "singing parakeet with undulating markings," and "Shaw" stands for the English naturalist George Shaw, who with Nodder first described the birds in 1805 in their book *Naturalists' Miscellany*.

The zoological classification of the parakeet is as follows:

Class: *Aves* (birds)
Order: *Psittaciformes* (parrots and allies)
Family: *Psittacidae* (parrots)
Subfamily: *Psittacinae* (true parrots)
Genus group: *Platycercini* (flat-tailed parrots)
Genus: *Melopsittacus* (singing parrots)
Species: *Melopsittacus undulatus* (parakeet or budgerigar)

Not all pairs are lucky enough to find such an ideal nesting cavity. Many have to make do with a hole among roots.

Subspecies (according to the Australian ornithologist Scoble): *M. u. intermedius* (northern budgerigar) and *M. u. pallidiceps* (western budgerigar).

This nomenclature, now used universally, goes back to the Swedish botanist Carlolus Linnaeus (1707–1778), whose system is based on the assumption that complex living organisms developed in the course of time from simpler organisms.

Parakeets at a Glance

Place of origin: Central Australia.
Habitat: Hot semi-deserts, arid and grassy savannas, especially along "creeks" (streams with intermittent flow).
Way of life: Always in groups; monogamous. Large flocks roam like nomads over wide areas in search of new feeding grounds.
Wild form: Green with yellow mask and wavy black-on-yellow lines on back of head, upper back, and wings.
Length: 7–9⅜ inches (18–24 cm) from the tip of bill over the head to the tip of the tail.
Tail: 3⅛–4½ inches (8–12 cm).
Weight: 1–1.4 ounces (30–40 g).
Life expectancy: 12 to 14 years.
Sexual maturity: At three to four months.
Breeding: After extensive rains.
Molt: Toward the end of a reproductive cycle.
Eggs per clutch: Four to six.
Egg laying: Every other day.
Beginning of incubation: After the first or second egg.
Incubation period: 18 days.
Nestling period: 28 to 32 days.

A Hot, Dry Country

Parakeets are found throughout the hot central section of Australia that makes up about

70 percent of the entire continent and is covered by grassy and scrub savannas. The birds always try to be near water and prefer nesting sites along the edge of eucalyptus forests or in the eucalyptus trees that grow along creeks—streams that carry water only intermittently but are often bordered by huge water eucalyptus trees.

In the tropical north of Australia, abundant rains fall in the summer and fall. In the south, the summers are hot and dry, with rain arriving only in the winter. The interior of the continent—where the parakeets live—lies between these two climatic zones and has no regular rainy seasons. Often there is no rain for months on end, sometimes even for years. At midday the temperature may rise to 104°F (40°C) in the shade or higher, and at night it sometimes drops below freezing. When this happens the parakeets fluff up their feathers and sleep huddled close together to keep warm. They are used to a 12-hour day because near the equator the sun rises within a few minutes shortly after 7:00 A.M. and sets just as quickly around 7:00 P.M. The birds fly to their sleeping trees every evening with noisy screeching. When the birds have all settled down, the trees look as though they were covered all over with flowers.

Living Like Nomads

Wild parakeets never live alone, but always in flocks of 20 to 40 and sometimes as many as 60 birds. A flock always inhabits an area where water is available within a few minutes of flying. Water is essential because the grass seeds and other kernels that make up a parakeet's diet contain very little moisture, and the birds have to drink frequently to soften them.

The birds fly together in a flock to the watering place and in search of food, and outside of the breeding period they also sleep together in communal sleeping trees. Mood changes spread from one bird to the entire flock. For example, if one parakeet is thirsty and sets off in the direction of the water source, the entire flock will quickly follow. However, if a bird has eaten its fill and wants to take off, a few others can dissuade the first one by taking off briefly with it but immediately landing and starting to eat again. The bird that is no longer hungry will then stay on with the rest of the flock. This is a good arrangement that helps protect the birds against predators. A single bird is an easier prey than one in a flock.

When food begins to get scarce in the flock's territory or the water source is about to dry up, the nomadic life begins. At first the parakeets spend several hours morning and evening flying over the territory that no longer yields sufficient sustenance. They rise higher every day, displaying their amazing flying skills. Thus, a flock will suddenly, in mid-flight, change direction without so much as one bird straying from its place in the formation. These flights are clearly different from the goal-oriented excursions in search of food and seem to serve the purpose of bringing the entire flock into a migrating mood.

Many ornithologists suspect that parakeets have an instinct that tells them where it is raining, for rain is synonymous with new feeding grounds, fresh water supplies, the production of offspring, and thus with survival. On their journey toward such a new "Eden," which is often hundreds of miles away, many flocks converge in huge superflocks of as many as 2,000 birds. Somehow they always manage to find areas where there is still water and grass with seeds. Later these superflocks break up again and each flock looks for its own range.

A Bond for Life

As soon as the rains come, the cocks start their courtship displays to arouse the hens' sexual instincts. If a hen is not interested in a suitor, she hacks at him angrily whenever he approaches. If, on the other hand, she takes a liking to him, she will bill and coo with him and let him feed her and scratch her head.

If a pair of parakeets forms a bond, it is usually for life, as in most other parrots. Only if a partner dies will there be reason to form a new bond. These monogamous bonds have the great advantage that the birds don't have to spend time finding partners when the rains start. At that point, time is precious because quite soon the half-ripe seeds necessary for raising a brood will be ready.

No Rain, No Offspring

Parakeets breed when it rains or after a prolonged rainfall. Rain brings not only water but also cooler weather and makes new grass sprout. The pairs immediately start looking for suitable nesting cavities, preferably in tall eucalyptus trees. One tree often accommodates eight pairs or even more. Birds unable to find a tree hole dig a hole among tree roots, make do with fallen tree trunks, or take over abandoned kingfisher nests. The male scouts for nesting cavities and shows them to his mate, who either accepts or rejects them. If a cavity is accepted, the hen spends days adapting and preparing the inside. She may enlarge the nest hollow and the entry hole by chipping at the wood with

her beak and smooth out the inside walls. All this is done in close proximity with other breeding pairs, for in the course of these activities the pairs mutually stimulate the courtship and breeding mood in each other. The first eggs will be laid very soon in the protective cavities because it is essential not to lose time. About 18 days after the first rainfall, tender grasses will have sprouted with half-ripe seeds—the ideal rearing food for baby parakeets.

Courtship, mating, incubation, and the nestling phase follow the same pattern in wild Australian parakeets as in our domesticated birds and are described in detail in the chapter Parakeet Offspring (pages 82–89). There is one difference, however. In the wild, the father is not allowed into the nesting cavity to feed the chicks until they have sprouted feathers. And once the nestlings can fly, the father hardly feeds them anymore. The young birds immediately start following their parents when they forage and learn to feed by imitating them. During the incubation period, the male calls the female to the entry hole and passes food to her. Once all the nestlings have feathers, the hen stops sitting on them. She begins to leave the nest frequently and joins the flock on its foraging flights.

Shortly before they are ready to leave the nest, the chicks, too, come to the entry hole to be fed and to get a good look at the world outside.

A Big Country

About one sixth of all the species of the parrot family—which includes our parakeets—live in Australia. The northern coast of this continent was discovered in 1606. The eastern coast was not explored until 1770. Northern Australia with its abundance of rain is rich in lush green forests, while savannas and deciduous trees dominate in most of the dry region in the continent's interior.

Flocks of parakeets range across the countryside in search of food.

On these journeys every stream and puddle of water is visited for refreshment.

The cock has discovered this cavity. Now the hen must decide whether it is appropriate for raising a family.

Molting Is Necessary

Parakeets in the Australian bush enter the molt toward the end of a breeding period and replace part of their plumage with new feathers. By the time the last nestlings have left, the parents' plumage is intact again, and the birds are ready to start on their long journey in search of new feeding grounds. If they don't breed over a long period because of the absence of rain, they usually molt during temperature fluctuations, but not much of the plumage is affected. Parakeets in the wild never replace all their feathers during a single molt because that would impair their flying ability too much and endanger their survival.

Everyday Life of Wild Parakeets

When the breeding season is over, the birds return to flock life, but the individual pairs maintain a close bond. All the birds rise up together to forage, especially in the morning and in the late afternoon. Their favorite food is half-ripe grass seeds. If there is no rain for a long time they eat dry seeds. Not only do they search for seeds along the ground, but they also climb up on plant stalks to reach them. Australian observers think that parakeets also eat small insects as the remains of insects have been found in the crops of some birds.

A flock flies to its watering place at least twice a day to drink. On hot days the birds need water about every three hours. Usually they take a few sips from the shallow shore, though some birds stand in the water up to their bellies when drinking. They also like to bathe in the shallow water, first dipping the head, then spreading the wings either both at once or one at a time, and splashing water onto the back. They can also satisfy their need for moisture by getting wet in the dewy grass when foraging in the early morning.

During the hot midday hours parakeets rest in shady tree tops, where they preen themselves, chirp softly, and are almost invisible to the observer.

From Soft Chirping to Loud Alarm Calls

The soft chirping during the resting periods induces a calm mood in the flock. It reassures the birds: "You're not alone; we're all here." The vocalizations of parakeets convey the dominant mood of the flock as well as specific information, and the birds even recognize individual voices by fine nuances in the utterances. On their long flights the birds periodically send calls that keep the flock together. When feeding, they are almost completely silent. Occasionally, a soft call can be heard, which probably expresses something like: "I'm here; where are you?" But when a bird emits a shrill alarm call, the flock responds instantaneously by rising up into the air.

Communication among breeding pairs is even more refined. It is necessary to safeguard individual distance. Respecting individual distance enables the birds to live so closely together in the colony with practically no outbursts of aggression.

Finally, vocal contact is essential between the parent birds to bring about the mutual agreement necessary for producing and rais-

ing offspring. It is this ability to produce highly differentiated sounds together with a very fine sense of hearing that is at the base of the talent parakeets have for learning a "foreign language" when they live with humans.

Predators

Parakeets have adapted amazingly well to their environment. Still, it is not easy for these small parrots to raise offspring. Like all animals living in the wild, they are surrounded not only by predators and competitors for food, but also by competitors for nesting sites. Australian swifts and a stocky, owl-like bird called the owlet nightjar sometimes rout parakeet females from their nesting cavities in order to nest there themselves.

Parakeet chicks that stick their heads out of the entry hole and beg vociferously for food also attract predatory birds. The pied butcherbird, for instance, pulls nestlings out through the nest hole and devours them. Snakes, too, attack brooding parakeets.

Parakeets are equipped with a number of defenses against predators. Their green coloring effectively camouflages them when they perch in shady trees, and their flying skills are spectacular. Even peregrine falcons, which specialize in flying prey, often miss in their attacks. As soon as the parakeets become aware of a raptor, they utter their alarm call and take off. Because they are able to change direction so fast in mid-air they generally escape their pursuers.

Parakeets have no effective way of shielding themselves from natural catastrophes like drought, heat, and brush fires. They try to make up for the losses—sometimes huge— caused by such disasters through rapid reproduction.

One other, major threat to these birds is man. Although parakeets are no longer killed for food—their former hunters, the aborigines, have long since adopted the white man's diet—wide sections of their habitat are disappearing because of economic and industrial development.

Parakeets As Pets

In the wild, a parakeet never lives by itself. The birds engage collectively in all activities, from the search for food to drinking. If a parakeet is kept singly as a pet, it forms a strong attachment to its people because of its need for companionship. In the absence of other birds, it regards humans as its "flock." A single parakeet requires a great deal of attention; it has to be talked to and played with so that its life in a human environment will not become too dull and depressing. If you recognize this responsibility and take it seriously, you will derive much pleasure from your bird. Still, keeping a pair is always much better for the bird's health and happiness.

A Bird Conquers Europe

The famous British naturalist John Gould first introduced Europe to parakeets, bringing back some skins in 1840, and later, live birds from Australia to England, where they caused great excitement. People immediately took to parakeets, even though they had no idea at first what clever, lively creatures these birds really are. In the early days parakeets were difficult to keep alive because no one really knew

what they ate, and in general, what their needs were.

Parakeets acquired instant popularity, but this popularity exacted a price that seems unconscionable today. Thousands upon thousands of birds perished on the long journey to Europe by sea. Those that survived generally did not live long in captivity because they were not fed and kept properly. Eventually, however, the efforts of aviculturists, aided by the vitality of the birds, showed results. People gradually figured out which seeds were good for the birds, and it was discovered by sheer accident that they are cavity breeders. A fancier had hung an empty coconut shell with an entry hole into the cage as a toy, which the female immediately took over for breeding and raising young.

Holland and Belgium were the import centers for parakeets at that time, and France alone soon needed 100,000 birds a year for its breeding station in Toulouse.

The white areas on the primaries form two bright bands when the wings are spread in flying.

In 1875 the first yellow parakeets were bred in Belgium, and in 1901 the first sky blue budgies made their debut—a development credited to a Dutchman. These blue birds were greatly admired, and some English fanciers paid huge prices for blue parakeets.

By the end of the nineteenth century Australia was forced to impose a strict embargo on the export of parakeets because the native stocks had been depleted to an alarming extent. By then, however, parakeets were bred so successfully in Europe that further imports were no longer essential.

In 1990 bird magazines and parakeet societies celebrated the 150th anniversary of the introduction of parakeets and honored breeders who contributed over the years to the success of pet parakeets since these small parrots first arrived in Europe. I myself am particularly grateful to those breeders who propagate

No one who has had the chance to watch wild parakeets in the air will want to restrict these skillful flyers to a cage all the time. A bird that is not allowed to fly is as miserable as, say, a goldfish kept in a canning jar.

parakeets with the goal of supplying bird lovers with healthy and lively pets. It is a hobby that makes nobody rich; at most it may yield a modest second income. These breeders must be as crazy about parakeets as I am.

The Parakeet as a Family Member

People who decide to purchase a pet parakeet usually want a lovable, lively, tame bird that talks. But parakeets don't naturally and automatically possess these qualities. You should be aware before you set out to the pet store or the breeder that it is entirely up to you whether the parakeet you are about to buy will remain shy and timid or will develop into a true member of the family. You will gain the bird's trust only if you are willing to spend lots of time with it and treat it very gently during the first weeks. Everyone else in the family should also be prepared to play with the parakeet and look out for potential dangers. Any healthy parakeet that joins human society at about six weeks is almost certain to become

tame if it is treated with enough love and affection.

Talking Is Not Everything

As "true parrots," parakeets are born with a talent for mimicking sounds, but this is no guarantee that a particular bird will learn to talk. Many learn to imitate the sound of the door bell, the ring of the telephone, a barking dog, a robin's song, or a person's cough. To do this, a bird has to feel comfortable and content in its surroundings, and it has to get lots of encouragement and stimulation. If a parakeet is motivated to talk it will soon try to articulate a few words and even say some short sentences. It is up to you whether your bird will stop here or whether it will enlarge its vocabulary. Spend time talking to your parakeet now, preferably always in the same setting, and repeat the same things over and over. Greet your bird every day with a "Good morning! How did you sleep?" and in the evening say "Good night. Time to go to sleep now."

A parakeet that is kept singly will not fly as enthusiastically as one with a partner because two birds keep urging each other on to ever new flying rounds. A single bird needs special attention and affection from its keeper, toward whom and after whom it will want to fly as much as possible.

A parakeet taking off on its rounds from a perch outside the cage.

Pairs make optimal use of the flying area.

If several parakeets are kept together in a sufficiently large room, having two landing platforms offers variety and can give rise to regular games of tag.

The undulating movement of the wings is evident in the downward stroke.

Chances are that the parakeet will soon produce an appropriate response, and a tradition will develop that the bird will sorely miss if it is broken.

A parakeet that produces the right words at the right time always evokes amazement and amusement, but a bird that expresses its desires without words but employs all its charm to get what it wants is just as winning. One such marvel was Maxi, a pied blue-and-white who whistled as well as any schoolboy and was a passionate "pianist." A boy in Maxi's family played the piano, and Maxi sat on his young friend's shoulder listening every day during practice session. Then, when he returned to his room, Maxi rushed to his toy piano, whose keys he could press down with his weight. He'd hop and dash across the keys as fast as he could and was visibly moved by the harmonies he produced.

A Happy Twosome

Whether a parakeet shares the home of a family where several people spend time with it and are potential friends, or whether it lives as an only bird in a close relationship with just one person, there will inevitably be times when it is left alone for a few hours and sometimes for days or even weeks. The keeper may be unhappy about this, but there is no way of explaining this to the bird. Being alone is something parakeets are not equipped to deal with because they are gregarious flock birds that form permanent pair bonds. In nature they are never alone. Their entire life is lived with a mate and in the midst of a flock.

A parakeet that is left alone too much pines. It may pluck its own feathers, become seriously ill, and even die. If, however, your bird has a companion of its own kind, it will not suffer so much from your "neglect." The two birds will have each other and will no longer feel lonely.

If kept properly, two compatible parakeets are happier than a single bird, even a well-loved one. They have no problems communicating

21

with each other, and they can make use of their entire range of behavior. There is always a true partner for all activities. A human partner is inadequate in many ways: People can't fly, don't sleep snuggled up next to the bird, don't eat in the cage, can't be fed by the bird, and are all thumbs when it comes to scratching their feathered friends. Two parakeets living together constantly spur each other on to activity: They move and fly a lot, and they keep looking for and finding new hiding places and perches.

If care is taken in introducing the second bird (see page 47), the objection that the first parakeet will lose interest in people and stop talking can be dismissed.

Should the Second Bird Be a Male or a Female?

It makes little difference whether the partner you select for your parakeet is of the same sex or not. What does matter is that the two birds are compatible. It is very rare for two parakeets to take a strong dislike toward each other that makes them chase and fight each other constantly. To be on the safe side, when you buy the second bird, you should ask the breeder for permission to return it if there is a problem. If two birds get along well, it doesn't matter whether they are the same sex or not. One of them will take on the role of the missing gender, and they will live together peacefully. You need only concern yourself with the sex of the second bird if you want your birds to produce offspring.

Important: Don't try to combine two females with one male. In this situation the females will fight to the death. Either keep true pairs or make sure all the birds are of the same sex.

Does a Parakeet Fit into My Life?

Here are ten points you should give some serious thought to before you get a parakeet:
1. The average life span of parakeets is 10 to 12 years. Are you willing to assume responsibility for a bird for this long? If you were to decide after a few years that you are tired of the bird and give it away it might die of grief.
2. Do you have a pleasant, permanent spot for the bird?
3. Are you willing to take good care of the bird even if, for whatever reason, it never becomes friendly or learns to talk?
4. Do you have enough time to devote to it? A parakeet needs daily care and it needs your company and attention several times a day.
5. A parakeet has to be able to fly and needs light and fresh air. In order to satisfy these needs without exposing it to danger the room has to be made bird-proof (see page 41).
6. A bird creates dirt. In spite of the cage bottom, which is supposed to catch the debris, seeds and chaff will still end up on the floor. During the molt the bird loses feathers, which are sent floating up at the slightest air movement. In addition, a parakeet produces droppings every 12 to 15 minutes wherever it happens to be sitting.
7. Are you a skier or sun lover and thus away a lot on weekends? You cannot regularly leave a bird alone for two days at a time.
8. What will happen to the bird when you go on vacation, have to travel for other reasons, or get sick? It is essential to find a reliable and loving substitute caretaker for the bird.
9. The bird may get sick. This means visits to the veterinarian, which are not cheap. Are you prepared for the extra expense?
10. Are you sure that no one in your family is allergic to feather dust? If you don't know, check with your doctor. Better to be safe than sorry. (See Warning, page 139.)

Fresh branches and green plants not only keep birds busy but are also a source of valuable nutrients.

When Max reads aloud, his bird wants to be right there.

Parakeets as Pets for Children

There are many children who wish they had a pet parakeet or who already have one. Growing up with a pet and taking care of it provides important experiences for children. It's the best way to learn what it means to assume a responsibility. However, a parakeet should never be bought just as a child's pet but should always be considered a "family bird," for which all the members of the family feel responsible.

If a parakeet were able to express itself in our language, it might describe a satisfying and happy day something like this:

Cindy's Story
I am a green parakeet female with markings like those of my wild cousins, and my name is Cindy. I've been living with Monica, Hans, and little Cathy for two months. They make up "my" flock. Cathy is especially nice about looking after me. She comes to my room in the morning before she goes off to school and says, "Good morning, Cindy. Cathy is going to bring you something good to eat." I always look forward to hearing her voice, and I answer by whistling since I don't know how to talk yet. While she fills my dishes with fresh seeds and water I sit on the highest perch in my cage and watch. At first I was afraid when her big hand reached into my cage. But she always talked to me so gently that I gradually lost my fear and even got brave enough to sit on her hand. She feeds me spray millet from her hand every day, and I like that.

After Cathy leaves for school, Monica comes in. She opens the door of my cage so that I can get out. First I fly around the room ten times, then I land on the bird tree, my favorite place to be. There I have a swing, a little bell, and many twigs to gnaw on. When Monica sits down at her desk I can finally fly to her and spend time on the desk, where there are so many interesting things. Monica sometimes tries to get me to leave. She throws little balls of paper at me, but I catch them in my bill and toss them to the floor. That's a great game! Monica has a lot of paper balls, and when she runs out of them, I spend the time it takes her to make new ones grooming myself all over. Usually Monica gives me some fruit or vegetables to eat. I especially like strawberries. Monica holds the berries for me so that I can pick off the little seeds. Then I take big bites and drink the juice.

Every afternoon Cathy gives me a little shower. At first I was supposed to dive into the water in my bath house, but I was afraid of that much water. So Cathy and I had the idea of giving me a shower with the spray bottle. I really enjoy that.

In the evening I sit on Hans's shoulder when he reads the paper. He often tells me stories then, and if he forgets I climb down his arm and yank on the paper a little.

When I get tired I settle down on my sleeping perch next to my mirror and stick my bill in my back feathers. I go to sleep quickly. But I wake up once more when Cathy comes to turn out the light and say "Good night." I am trying to learn to say it, too, and when I know how I'll say "Good night" to her.

The small berries are very tasty but they have to be held up to the bird so that it can bite into them.

Parakeets Are Lovable Pets

Over the years many children have told me about their parakeets. Let me quote from a few of the letters:

• Erica writes: "I like to play with my parakeet. When I get home from school he is already waiting for me, and we play with the little ball made of plastic ribs he likes so much. I roll it along the floor and he races after it. When he gets worn out dashing around, he settles down on my shoulder and snuggles up to me as close as he can."

• "I can tell my parakeet all my secrets," Monica writes. "He sits on my hand and listens to everything I say with a very understanding look. He has often made me feel better."

• Max reports: "My two parakeets are veritable acrobats. When I come into the room they perform their acts for me on the bird tree. I built the tree myself together with my dad."

A Parakeet for a Child

If you decide to get a parakeet for your child, include the child in the preparations. Tell him or her about how parakeets live in the wild, how they choose mates for life, raise their young, and what sociable creatures they are. Explain that a parakeet does not understand who "owns" him and will respond to the person who treats him gently, is around a lot, plays with him, and takes care of his needs. Draw up a list with the child of the things that need to be done before the parakeet arrives, and discuss how the chores can best be divided among all the family members.

Children up to seven years can give the parakeet a little treat at a regular time every day once the bird has become used to its new

The best toy of all is a small ball made of plastic ribs... | ...but even paper can provide entertainment.

home. The bird will look forward to this and quickly regard the young donor as a likable member of his flock.

Children seven to ten years of age can be entrusted with purchasing the bird's food and may occasionally buy a small toy with their own money. Depending on their physical coordination they may also be asked to clean the cage if it is not too heavy. The children should at least help with the weekly cleaning.

Children ten or older can look after their parakeet without adult help. But the parents should still check to make sure that the bird gets enough to eat and that there are always seeds and water in its dishes. They should also observe the bird every day in order to detect any sign of impending illness.

Very important: Ask your child to tell you everything he or she notices about the bird. Ask about its talent for talking or whistling, what it likes to play with, its favorite food, whether it has a permanent sleeping place or a favorite perch. Only if you show a continuing interest will the child be motivated to observe the bird closely.

Children Make Toys for Their Parakeet
A parakeet needs a few toys to keep it from getting bored. These can be bought at a pet shop, but it's more fun—and cheaper—to

make them yourself.

Tassels of hemp rope keep birds occupied because they like to peck at the rope and pull on the strands. Use only undyed hemp. Cut 15 to 20 strands about 6 inches long, fold them in half, and tie the folded end tightly about ¾ inch (2 cm) from the end with another piece of hemp rope to hold the strands together. Take another piece of rope, run it through the loop thus created, and use it to tie the tassel to the cage roof or a branch of the bird tree.

A swing is also easy to construct. You need a branch about 4 inches (10 cm) long and ½ to ¾ inch (1.2–2 cm) thick, two pieces of wire about 10 inches (25 cm) long, and some undyed hemp rope. First scrub the branch with warm water and rub it dry. Then wrap one end of the wires twice around the ends of the branch, and bend the other ends of the wires so that they can easily be hooked on the bars of the cage top. But before hanging the swing in the cage you have to wrap the wires with hemp rope so that the bird can't get hurt on them. Renew the rope wrapping from time to time because the bird will no doubt peck at it.

Wooden curtain rings can also be wrapped in hemp rope and tied to the cage bars or to the bird tree with rope or string. Birds like to whet their bills on the rings or use them to swing on.

Golden Rules for Young Parakeet Owners

If you are given a parakeet, you have been entrusted with something very precious. A parakeet is an intelligent creature and will watch you very closely. At first it will probably be shy and fearful, but the better it gets to know you the friendlier it will become—as long as you don't frighten it. If you observe the following rules, you will soon have a tame bird.

• Offer it a small treat every day at the same time. But first you have to figure out what the bird likes to eat.

• Never go up to the cage without talking to the bird. All birds are afraid of silent creatures.

• If you have to reach into the cage, keep talking soothingly to the bird.

• Go up to the cage several times a day and get close enough that the bird can see you well. Talk to it. Say its name several times, and softly sing or whistle a little tune for it.

• When you let the bird out of the cage to let it fly free, make sure all doors and windows are closed. Otherwise, the parakeet might escape.

• When the bird is allowed to fly outside the cage, don't try to touch it or pick it up because that would scare it. If it comes to you of its own free will and sits on your hand or shoulder, the bird is in the mood for contact, and you can try to play with it or pet it gently.

• Once the bird feels comfortable with you, you can try scratching it very gently. Take the shaft of a feather the bird has shed and run it over its head a few times. If the bird doesn't move away, you can move the feather over the bird's head very gently in the other direction, so that its feathers stand up. If the bird likes this, it will come more and more often to be scratched in this way.

• And last but not least: Always remember that there is nothing worse for a parakeet than to be left alone. If you leave the house, take the bird to a room where there is another person or bird.

Anything that glitters and shines fascinates parakeets.

A Bird Joins
Your Household

You should have completed all the necessary preparations before you set out for the pet store or the breeder to select and bring home your new family member. The separation from its fellows, being captured, the journey in the small box, and, finally, the completely strange environment in which the little bird finds itself are all traumatic experiences from which it can recover rapidly only if calm returns and there are no further upsetting events.

Therefore, you should decide beforehand on the best place for the cage and make whatever changes may be necessary in the room. Install a permanent screen in a window (see page 41) now so there will be no danger of escape when you want to air the room.

The cage, too, should be all ready and set up for the bird's comfort (see How-to: The Cage, pages 34 and 35) so that you won't have to make changes later and frighten the newly arrived bird.

The Right Place for the Cage

The cage can be a place of safety for a parakeet only if it is left alone and not moved around. Birds feel secure in a cage; that is where they can eat, drink, and sleep in peace.

The best place for a cage is the living room, or wherever the family members spend most of their time. Your parakeet will be comfortable if its cage is in a bright corner near a window. Set the cage on a sturdy shelf securely mounted on the wall at adult eye level. The space above the cage should be empty because parakeets are frightened by activities going on above their heads.

Absolutely no drafts should reach the location of the cage. Drafts can make parakeets ill. Check how draft-free a place is with a lit candle. The flame will flicker at air currents that are imperceptible to us.

Tip: If you're going to have a party or it's time for major housecleaning, move the bird with its cage to another room.

A perch outside the cage offers a good landing place after flying around the room.

If a pair of parakeets is kept uncaged in a bird-proof room, the birds keep motivating each other to fly. This is very beneficial to their health and vitality.

If a cat gets a hold of as much as the tail of a bird, that's the end of the bird.

Inappropriate Locations:
• Immediately in front of a window: Windows radiate too much cold in the winter, and in the summer birds can suffer heat stroke if exposed to the direct sun.

• In the kitchen: There are many potential dangers in a kitchen, such as harmful vapors, smoke, hot stove burners, pots and dishes with liquid or hot contents, detergents, and other cleaning agents. In addition, airing the kitchen creates drafts.

• In a child's room: It's too boring for the bird there because most children spend very little time in their rooms. Often they only go there to do their homework.

A Short Shopping List for the Initial Furnishings

• A millet spray. This is both a special treat and a highly nutritious food.

• A mineral block or a cuttlebone with a clamp to attach it to the cage. There should be a label with the mineral block to the effect that it contains all the substances necessary for strengthening bones and forming new feathers. These substances are naturally present in cuttlebone.

• A bath house that can be hung into the open cage door. It should have a textured bottom so that the bird won't slip when bathing.

• Medicinal charcoal, in case the transport and the change in environment cause diarrhea. If needed, sprinkle a little of the charcoal over the birdseed or, better yet, on a slice of apple. However, the necessity of a daily supply of charcoal is questionable as it is suspected of absorbing vitamins A, B_2, and K from the intestinal tract. If this is correct, it can mean that charcoal can cause vitamin-deficiency diseases.

• One or two extra food dishes that can be hung on the bars of the cage for offering fruit, vegetables, and sprouted seeds.

• A water dispenser or bottle, if you like. The water stays cleaner in these devices than in an open cup. Offer water in the cup as well as the automatic dispenser or bottle until the bird has gotten used to the latter.

• A small bell and a mirror to be hung in the cage. These items will help comfort a single bird after the separation from its fellows.

• Bird sand for the cage floor. The sand fulfills not only a hygienic function but is also necessary for the bird's health.

Important: Remember when you pick up the bird to also take home a package of the birdseed mixture it is accustomed to.

Where You Can Buy Parakeets

You will find parakeets in a wide selection of colors in pet stores and in well-run pet sections of department stores. If you can't find a bird that really appeals to you in any store, contact a bird breeder club (for addresses see page 138) and ask if there is a parakeet breeder in your area. Or you may get an address from your closest animal shelter.

If you go to cage bird shows where breeders exhibit their birds, you can not only get addresses there but also find out when a breeder next expects to have young birds.

Tip: When you select a parakeet either in a pet store or at a breeder's, be sure to take your time and look carefully at the establishment. Unfortunately, every branch of trade has its few black sheep. Observe whether the birds live in overly crowded quarters, how clean everything is, whether the air in the room is fresh, and whether the birds are lively and active.

Age of Birds at Purchase

At the age of five to eight weeks, parakeets usually adjust without problems to a new environment and to their new caretakers. You can tell a youngster by its large, black "button" eyes, in which the white iris around the pupil does not yet show. The barring on the head extends down to the cere, the throat spots are still small or hardly show up at all, and the bill is darker than that of an adult parakeet. The band on the bird's foot has the year of birth stamped on it, but that doesn't tell you when in that year the bird was born and, consequently, how many weeks it has been alive. The purchase, therefore, always contains an element of trust, for young parakeets keep their same appearance until their first molt at around three months.

Note: Fledgling parakeets about four weeks old adjust to a change of home especially quickly. But often birds this young are only available directly from the breeder. You may ask your pet dealer to facilitate a purchase directly from a breeder. Of course, you have to make sure that the young bird can eat without help from its parents.

What a Healthy Parakeet Looks Like

• All the feathers hug the body smoothly and have a muted sheen.

• The feathers around the vent are not stuck together or dirty with excreta.

• Eyes and nostrils are not runny or encrusted with dried secretion.

• The horny scales on the feet and toes lie flat.

• Two of the four toes on the feet point forward, the other two backward. If a toe is missing, this is a physical flaw but it is not a sign of illness.

• The bird moves around in a lively manner, grooms itself periodically, and is in active contact with its fellows.

A sick parakeet sits off to the side apathetically. Its plumage is slightly puffed up, and the eyes are half shut. The bill is buried in the back feathers. Look at the bird again a few minutes later because it might just have been asleep earlier.

Male or Female?

This question is irrelevant if you buy only one parakeet. Males can become just as friendly as females. Temperament and the ability to learn

The taller the bird tree, the better the birds like it, but toys can make the lower levels attractive, too.

are not linked to gender. You can tell the sex of an adult parakeet by the color of its cere, the waxy-looking area at the base of the upper mandible where the two nostrils are located. The cere is bright blue in the male and beige or brownish to brown in the female. The blue of the male's cere becomes more intense when the adult bird enters the courtship mood. In weak or sick birds, the blue of the cere can fade, and with advancing age, the cere of the male sometimes turns brownish. The cere of the female also changes when the bird enters the breeding condition. The color darkens, and in some individuals the cere takes on a somewhat shriveled look. In young birds of both sexes the cere is still a pale pink or beige. Thus, you can never be quite sure when you buy a fledgling parakeet whether you are taking home a male or a female.

A Single Bird or a Pair?

I am a strong advocate of keeping pairs. But I would start out with one bird, get it acclimated and tame, and offer it the freedom of a bird-proof room (see page 41). Only then would I get it a companion. If you buy two parakeets at the same time, the birds will not become tame. They are so preoccupied with each other that they won't accept a human being as a partner. You can read on page 47 how to acclimate the second bird. Keeping a pair of parakeets is more in tune with the birds' natural way of life. Furthermore, you will feel less guilty if you occasionally have no time for your birds (see pages 21 and 22). Two birds living together don't get lonely, even if you are not around. Still, they are happy when you return, for then the flock, of which you are part, is complete once again.

Choosing the Color

Parakeets are bred in more than 100 different varieties. Many of these are rather rare and found only in birds belonging to breeders. The general pet trade offers green, blue, white, yellow, and pied parakeets, with some variations in color intensity. There are also "opaline" birds with a V-shaped area on the back where there are no markings. You can choose among these colors according to your taste, but I would especially recommend green or blue birds because they are far more robust than the rarer color varieties.

Different Pets

Parakeets and dogs generally get along fine if the dog is obedient and is not neglected because of the arrival of the new pet. Cats and parakeets are a different story and are unlikely to coexist peacefully. Hamsters, guinea pigs, and dwarf rabbits also should not be kept in the same room with a parakeet because they may bite it or infect it with parasites.

Check the Band

It is recommended that all parakeets wear a closed coded band on the foot. This can be a closed ring put on by the breeder when the bird is between five and ten days old or an open metal band, the so-called split band, which is placed on the foot later on. In the United States the band is not legally required, but if a bird has one it serves as a permanent means of identification and documents the bird's origin. It is important to check the banded foot regularly. If the bird gets the band caught on anything, it will pull frantically and can hurt itself. If the leg swells up, the band may cut off circulation and will have to be removed by a veterinarian. If that happens, ask the vet for a written statement explaining that the band was removed for medical reasons and keep this statement as well as the band.

How-to: The Cage

Even if you start out with one parakeet, you should already be thinking about the possibility of getting a second one. By its very nature this gregarious little Australian bird will be happier living with one of its own kind than having to depend entirely on the love of humans for the satisfaction of its social needs.

The Right Parakeet Cage

We recommend that you start out with a cage that is large enough for two parakeets.

Minimum dimensions: 20 inches long, 12 inches deep, 18 up on them. The bars should be no more than ½ inch (12 mm) apart.

Cage accessories: The standard equipment usually includes a bottom tray with a plastic sand drawer, two food dishes for birdseed and water, perches, and, sometimes, a swing.

Get also a bath house, clamps to hold millet sprays and greens, a mineral block, additional food dishes, and bird sand.

A Play Area on Top of the Cage
Photo 1
You can buy mini playgrounds

The Perches
Photo 2
The plastic or dowel perches that come with the cage should be replaced with natural branches ½ to ¾ inch (1.2–2 cm) thick. The birds will happily go to work on these new perches with their beaks.

Important: The branches should be thick enough for the bird's toes to just barely reach around and meet.

Mounting: The number of branches should not exceed the number of perches that were originally present in the cage.

1. Parakeet playgrounds like this one, which can easily be mounted on a cage roof, are sold at pet stores.

2. Natural branches make healthy perches for parakeets.

inches high (50 x 30 x 45 cm). Keep in mind that a cage this size will accommodate the birds only for eating and sleeping.

Ideal dimensions: 40 inches long, 20 inches deep, 32 inches high (100 x 50 x 80 cm).

The bars: The bars along the long sides have to run horizontally so that the birds can climb

for birds at pet stores. This type of playground can be mounted on top of the cage very simply, where it will serve as a play area and landing site outside the cage for one or two parakeets. Bunches of greens or fresh branches—preferably hazelnut or willow—offered there will keep the birds busy.

Birds like not only horizontal perches but also ones that are at a slant. Cut all branches to the proper length, make notches in both ends, and squeeze them between the bars.

Nonpoisonous Twigs and Branches

Suitable kinds: Oak, alder,

elderberry, chestnut, basswood, poplar, and willow.

Important: Don't pick branches from trees and bushes along roads with a lot of traffic.

Cleaning: Scrub all branches with hot water and let dry before you let the bird near them.

Many pet shops sell natural branches, often already cut to proper size for use in cages.

Extra Food Dishes
Photo 3
One food dish each for birdseed and water is not enough for two parakeets because, as soon as one begins to eat or drink, the other will want to do the same. You will also need some additional dishes for fresh food. Buy dishes that can be hung on the cage bars near the perches. You can also hang small baskets made of untreated natural materials on the cage bars.

Important: Place the food cups where no droppings can reach them.

Automatic food and water dispensers: The waterers available at pet stores are excellent because they keep the water free from dirt. If you get an automatic food dispenser you have to check it frequently and remove the empty seed husks that accumulate in the feeding trough so that the bird can get at the whole seeds.

Practical Clamps
Photo 4
Pet stores sell practical metal clamps for attaching entire millet

3. A little basket is used as an extra dish for fresh foods.

sprays, bunches of greens, and similar foods to the cage wall. These clamps keep these foods from dropping to the cage floor. There are also clamps for smaller pieces of millet spray. Wooden clothespins are also helpful for clamping "treats," such as greens and millet spray, to the trellis of the cage.

Important: Keep your birds from gorging on these special treats or they will be reluctant to eat their regular food.

Miniature Meadows
Photo 5
These, too, can be purchased at pet stores. They consist of grasses that are good for parakeets. Buy a small pot of soil with seeds that are ready to sprout. When the grass dies, you can get refills.

The Bird Sand
Spread about ⅜ inch (1 cm) of the sand or corncob litter on the bottom of the cage. It will absorb liquid and keep the cage sanitary. Sand is also an indispensable aid to digestion. The birds keep eating a little sand and grit, which helps break down the seeds in the gizzard.

4. Special clamps for cuttlebone and spray millet.

Important: Never buy a so-called bird carpet or perch cover. This is bird sand glued to cardboard. It comes in flat pieces and in small rolls that fit over the perches. When the birds peck at

5. A miniature meadow in a plastic box offers a lasting supply of fresh greens and is highly recommended.

the sand, they may swallow other parts of the carpet that may make them sick or even cause death.

Tip: If your bird refuses to eat sand off the cage bottom, offer sand in a separate cup or sprinkle it over the fresh food.

How-to: A Perch Outside the Cage

A perch in the open is an ideal addition to the cage. A bird tree or a hanging perch will quickly become the parakeets' favorite spot. The birds will use it as a take-off point for flights around the room, for resting, and for doing gynmastics.

Branches and Twigs for the Perch

Select the branches you will use to construct the perch carefully.

Suitable kinds are: Oak, alder, elderberry, chestnut, basswood, poplar, willow, hazelnut, and unsprayed fruit trees.

Warning: Never use branches…

• from nurseries—these trees have generally been treated with pesticides,

• from trees growing near roads—they have been exposed to exhaust fumes,

• from commercial orchards —these trees are regularly sprayed with pesticides.

Important: Scrub the twigs

and branches under hot water and let them dry before letting the birds near them.

Building a Bird Tree

Photos 1 to 5
You will need…

• a round or square tub measuring at least 20 inches (50 cm) across,

• a cast-iron Christmas tree stand,

• a sturdy, fairly straight branch 6 feet (2 m) long or longer, preferably with a few side branches,

• several smaller branches of varying thicknesses (½ to ¾ inch [1.2–2 cm]),

• 10 to 15 cobblestones, about fist size,

• fresh garden or potting soil,

• 6 to 10 pounds (3–5 kg) bird sand,

• 1 to 3 rolls of florist's wire,

• undyed hemp rope.

Planting the trunk of the bird tree: Put the bottom end of the large branch in the Christmas

tree stand and screw it in tightly. Place the stand in the middle of the tub (Photo 1).

Filling the tub: Place the cobblestones in the tub so that they cover the tree stand and keep the tree standing straight (Photo 2). Cover the stones and fill the spaces between them with soil. Top the well packed soil with about 1½ inches (4 cm) of bird sand (Photo 3).

Adding side branches: Hold the side branches (½ to ¾ inch [1.2–2 cm] thick) up against the trunk the way they are going to be and cut them to size so that none of them stick out beyond the tub's edge. This way droppings and other debris will land in the tub rather than on the floor.

Attaching the branches: If your main branch already has a side branch, attach another branch there, laying it in the fork. Tightly wrap florist's wire around the main stem, the original branch, and the branch you are

1. Place the tree stand with the main stem of the tree in the tub.

2. Fill the tub with fist-sized stones.

3. Add soil and top with about 1¼ inches (4 cm) of bird sand.

4. Attach side branches to the main stem with wire.

5. Wrap a thick layer of undyed hemp rope around the wire.

adding. To make sure the birds won't hurt themselves on the wire, cover it with a thick layer of undyed cord (photos 4 and 5). Attach other branches at different heights to create different levels

Note: You will have to replace the cord periodically because the birds like to nibble on it.

Tip: If the branch that forms the trunk of the bird tree has no natural side branch, tie two branches of about the same thickness horizontally to the main stem with wire, and then wrap the place with cord.

The Location of the Bird Tree

Place the tree as far from the cage as possible so that the birds will have to fly quite a bit to get back and forth every time they want to eat or drink. This keeps them fit. A spot near a window is ideal. If the window has a screen the birds can also enjoy the fresh air on warm days.

A Hanging Perch

Photo 6

This perch requires no shelf and satisfies the birds' need to perch as high up as possible. You will need…

• a board about ⅝ inch (1.5

cm) thick of untreated wood (24 inches long and 16 inches wide [60 x 40 cm]),

• 4 wooden slats (2 inches [5 cm] wide, ³⁄₁₆ inch [.5 cm] thick),

• 8 thin wood screws,

into a frame, then set the frame on the board and glue it on or attach it with screws from the bottom.

Adding branches: Cut the two branches to size so they won't extend beyond the bottom tray. Cut the chain to the right lengths and add a key ring at each end. Hook a screw eye to each ring, and screw the screw eyes into the frame of the tray and to the branches in such a way that the tray hangs horizontally below the branches.

Placing the hanging perch: The perch should be low enough for you to reach it comfortably

6. A hanging platform consisting of a tray of untreated wood to catch the dirt and, above the tray, a couple of natural branches that serve as perches. The platform is hung from the ceiling by means of a screw anchor, a hook-eye screw, and a spring safety hook.

• 10 to 12 small screw eyes,

• 10 to 12 small key rings,

• 2 natural branches of different thicknesses,

• about 5 feet (1.5 m) of light metal chain.

Tray to catch droppings: Screw the wooden slats together

for cleaning. Attach a chain of appropriate length to the middle of the upper branch so that the tray will balance in a horizontal position. Then hang the entire affair from the ceiling, using a screw anchor, a large screw eye, and a spring safety hook.

Gentle Acclimation

The best way to help your parakeet adjust to life with you is to take advantage of its love for regular routines. Parakeets like their days to take a predictable course—everything should always happen the same way. They are upset by change, and anything new has to be introduced slowly. Keep this in mind, especially during the first phase of your life together.

Try to avoid anything that might frighten your parakeet. It is now up to you whether your bird will perceive its new world positively or negatively. Once the bird starts eating some seeds, drinks a little, and preens itself, it has taken a big step toward adjusting to its new environment.

The First Few Hours at Home

You have brought your parakeet home in its little box, protecting it on the way from cold and heat and taking the quickest possible route. Now you want the bird to get used to its new home as soon as possible and to overcome the sadness caused by the separation from its fellows. Hold the open box in front of the cage door in such a way that the bird has

no choice but to enter the cage. It will be happy to move from the darkness of the box into the brighter light. At first it may want to withdraw into a corner, the way it used to react as a nestling when it was frightened.

Once the parakeet is in the cage, close the door and leave the bird alone. This way it will most quickly muster the courage to take a look around, eat, and drink. But don't bother it even if it hardly eats at all at first. It will make up for lost time later on. What is important at this point is to try to avoid doing anything that might frighten the bird.

Many parakeets get used to their new surroundings quite quickly. Thus, one parakeet owner wrote to me: "Our green parakeet, Pepi, was just six weeks old when we got him. Everything was set up and ready for him. He fled from the transport box into his cage and immediately climbed onto the swing, which for many years remained his favorite place. For two days he hardly moved at all and barely ate. After that he developed a healthy appetite, tested all the perches in the cage with his beak, and kept setting the little bell ringing. The spell was broken." There are also

If the bird tree offers both green plants and fruit, the birds hardly know what to taste first.

If there is birdseed available on the bird tree as well, the cage will be empty most of the time.

Even if your birds are free to roam in the room all the time, you should lure them back to the cage with a treat once a day so they won't abandon it altogether. There are times when the birds are safest in their cage.

parakeets that take much longer to adjust to their new home. Let your bird take its time. Keep saying its name from the first day on, and speak soothingly to it whenever you approach. This way it will get used to your voice. It will learn its name and learn not to be afraid of you. Almost all parakeets are naturally afraid of creatures that approach silently. During the first few days you will want to speak to your new pet from a distance and preferably sitting down in a spot where the bird can watch you.

Keep Away Fear of the Dark

Leave a little light on in the bird room for the first few nights so that the bird will quickly realize where it is if an unusual noise startles it at night. If it's completely dark, birds can panic and flutter wildly about the cage, possibly injuring themselves. For this same reason you should not cover the cage with a cloth. Covering the cage makes sense only if there is a bright street lamp outside the window that would disturb the bird's rest or if someone has to work late in the same room.

Once the bird has gotten used to its new surroundings and the sounds that are part of them, you no longer have to leave on a light at night. But for nervous birds that scare easily I recommend leaving on a small night light even after the bird has adjusted. Night lights shed a very dim light and are plugged directly into an outlet.

The First Morning

Remember to talk to the bird when you enter its room on the first morning to take the food dishes out of the cage. Always accompany everything you do near the bird with soothing words because the little creature is bound to be afraid when your big hand comes uncomfortably close for the first time. Remain very calm; don't let the bird's nervousness affect you. On the first morning all that is necessary is to put fresh seed in the food cup and change the water. There will be only a few droppings on the bottom of the cage, so you can wait until the next day to pull out the sand drawer to remove them and the seed hulls with a spoon.

Surely it must be possible to put a notch in this branch?

A Bird-proof Room

The biggest danger for parakeets is flying away. These skillful long-distance flyers are drawn as though by a magnet to the fresh air. They know instinctively that outside the window there is unlimited space for flying. What they do not know is that the outdoors is not a suitable environment for them and harbors countless dangers, and they do not know that they will not find their way back to safety, because as pet birds they have not developed the ability to orient themselves by features of the landscape. That is why it is so important to have a safe screen in at least one window section that opens. The screen should be made of sturdy wire mesh (width between wires $3/8$ to $3/4$ inch [1–2 cm]) stretched over a wooden frame that is screwed into the window opening. With the window thus protected you can air the room any time without worrying that your bird might escape.

Human living quarters contain other dangers to parakeets as well, dangers that have to be recognized and, as far as possible, eliminated. Check in the glossary at the back of this book whether any of your houseplants are poisonous or harmful for parakeets (see Poisonous Plants, page 131) because it is practically impossible to keep the birds from nibbling on plants. It is advisable in general to keep only inexpensive and fast-growing plants in a bird room, and to keep them alive by exchanging them periodically with others.

Watch out for Danger

As already mentioned, an apartment contains many potential dangers for a parakeet.

Bathroom: If the window is open even a crack, the bird may escape. It can also drown in an uncovered toilet. Keep the bathroom door closed, and let the bird in only if you are there, too.

Bookshelves: If a bird gets behind the books, it will not be able to get out again without help. Therefore, all the books should be pushed flush against the wall. You can also provide openings by laying a couple of books flat every couple of feet.

Containers with water: The bird may slip into a bucket—mistaking suds for a solid landing surface—or into a vase or a large glass,

and drown. Cover all containers, and don't let your bird fly free while you clean house.

Closets and drawers: The bird may hide without your noticing it and will suffocate or starve if not rescued. Never leave closets or drawers open, not even a crack.

Open doors: A bird can get squashed when the door closes. Get used to closing all doors very cautiously.

Poisons: Fatal poisoning can be caused by alcohol, pencil lead, the tips of ballpoint and fountain pens, strong spices, glues, plant fertilizer, cleansing materials, and so on. All such things should be stored out of reach of the birds, and all traces of these substances should be carefully removed.

Cooking stove: A bird can suffer fatal burns if it lands on a hot burner. Always place a pan with cold water on hot burners, and never let the birds fly unsupervised in the kitchen.

Candle light: A bird can also suffer fatal

Dogfood doesn't taste too bad, but spray millet is still preferred by birds.

burns if it flies though a candle flame. Do without candle light if your bird is flying free in the room.

Wastebaskets and ornamental vessels: Birds can slip in and then are unable to climb out again without help. Death caused by starvation or a heart attack brought on by fright may be the result. Use woven baskets or line wastebaskets with wire mesh. Ornamental vessels can be filled with sand.

Direct sun, overheated cars: Birds can die of heart attack or heat stroke. Look for a shaded parking spot, and manage to allow air into the car.

Temperature fluctuations: Abrupt changes in temperature can cause colds or heat stroke. Acclimate your bird gradually to temperatures between 41 and 77°F (5–25°C).

Flypaper: The parakeet may get stuck on it and become so frightened that it suffers a heart attack. Do not hang flypapers in rooms the bird spends time in.

Insect sprays: Do not use these in the vicinity of the bird because they are toxic to birds or can cause suffocation.

Sharp objects: Ends of wire, nails, splinters, needles, and such things are dangerous for birds because they can cause cuts and punctures. Try not to leave any sharp objects lying around but store them instead in a place that is inaccessible to the birds.

The First Free Flight
How long a newly arrived parakeet should stay exclusively in its cage depends primarily on the bird's temperament. With a shy and easily frightened bird, it is best to wait two to three weeks before letting it explore the room for the first time. A lively, curious bird, on the other hand, can be let out as early as the third or fourth day—under careful supervision, of course, so that you can step in if help is needed. The first time the cage door is left open your parakeet will either emerge from its home immediately and fly off or it may sit for a while, undecided, in the door opening. But at some point even a cautious bird will take off, as the longing for freedom is stronger than fear.

More difficult than taking off is landing, for the many unfamiliar objects in the room are intimidating. If the bird does not succeed in alighting on top of its cage, it will no doubt seek out some other spot high up; the higher it can perch, the safer it feels. Having once found such a spot, many parakeets on their first expedition out of the cage don't then dare leave it. If this is the case, hold the cage up as close to the bird as you can. This may give the bird the necessary courage. If you can't reach the bird because it is too high up, leave it there and don't worry, even if it spends the night there. The next morning hunger and thirst will motivate it to return to its cage. If the bird has landed on the floor, sprinkle a few seeds there for it; parakeets like to forage on the ground. If, after a while, you put the cage next to the bird it will probably be happy to climb back in.

"We Could Call Him Charley"

There are no limits when it comes to naming your parakeet. John or Jane, Bill or Betty might do, but surely you can do better. Why not call a pair Bogart and Bacall? And your blonde female Madonna? An aggressive, pushy sort could be Caesar, and shy, retiring type, Casper.

If one bird is already on the perch...

...landing calls for precision navigating.

Very important: If your bird is reluctant to return to its cage, don't ever try to chase after it, reach for it, or catch it in flight. This would scare the bird half to death, and whatever trust in you it had developed would be destroyed. Even a tame parakeet should be grasped only if emergency help is needed.

The Danger of Windowpanes
Before you open the cage door you should shut all doors and windows and draw the cur-

tains, for birds don't recognize that windows are like walls. Your bird might crash full force into a window and break its neck or suffer a concussion.

If your windows don't have curtains, lower a shade, leaving only about 8 inches (20 cm) of the window uncovered, and turn on all the lights. Increase the uncovered space a couple of inches every day, until the bird has grasped that the window is a solid wall. This usually takes just a few days, and the bird will then probably recognize the solid nature of windows in other rooms as well.

Getting Used to the Hand
During the first few days you have to proceed with great caution when approaching your parakeet and give it time to observe its surroundings in peace from the cage. Very soon, though, the bird will start to show pleasure at seeing you in the morning and will answer your greetings with happy twittering. Now you should start working on hand-taming your bird.

First step: As soon as the bird no longer flutters wildly or withdraws fearfully into a corner when you reach into the cage you can try to gently stroke your finger over its abdomen or its bill while talking soothingly. The bird will then learn that your hand is not dangerous.

Second step: After a few days stop leaving spray millet in the cage but offer it instead from your hand every day at the same time. First hold this treat in such a way that the bird can get at it without touching you. Continue to offer the millet this way even if the bird is too timid to actually get at it.

Third step: At some point the parakeet will stretch its neck out far enough to actually pick a few seeds from the spray. Then it will get a little closer every day to be able to eat more of the millet. Now it's time to place the millet spray on your open hand, so that the bird is forced to place a foot on your hand. Once you have reached this point it won't be long before the bird will hop onto your hand without thinking twice about it.

Aids to facilitate adjustment: Watch your parakeet; sometimes the bird itself will give

One of the two birds always seems to be in the air, where some look more elegant than others.

Parakeets clean and groom every single feather painstakingly. For, in nature, keeping the plumage in perfect shape is crucial for survival. If, for instance, a predator approaches, the bird has to be able to take to the air instantly.

Gnawing on branches is fine, but picking apart and unraveling hemp rope is even more fun.

you a hint of how it might get used to you more easily. I did everything I described above when my parakeet Manky first arrived—with limited success. What finally made the difference was his bell. For a long time this bell was the only thing Manky cared about, for before joining our household Manky had been one of those solitary pets that lives without much attention or love from its owner. The first few weeks he lived with me he was so petrified that he barely dared breathe when I was nearby. His cage stood on my desk, so that he could see me from morning till night, and he gradually got accustomed to my presence. Every so often this usually quiet, shy bird would be seized by a temper tantrum, and he would pull with all his might on the chain his bell hung on. This happened once when I happened to be there to give him fresh food, and the bell fell to the cage floor. Manky was

Be sure to cut off the long fibers your parakeets pull from the rope as soon as you notice them. Birds can easily strangle themselves on them. For the same reason, you should not hang toys from long pieces of rope.

visibly upset by this mishap. I picked up the bell to hang it up again, but Manky could not wait to be close to his beloved object again and jumped onto my hand. I slowly pulled the bell across my hand, up my arm, and let it dangle from my shoulder. Manky followed the bell and found himself sitting on my shoulder for the first time. From then on I made a point of wearing a small bell on the collar of my dress, so that Manky had a choice between two bells. Soon he found the one he could reach from my shoulder more attractive.

First Signs of Trust

Watch carefully to see how your parakeet reacts when you enter the bird room and call its name. The parakeet will soon express its pleasure at seeing you by briefly raising both wings or answering you with a brief call. It may shake its feathers vigorously to express relief at seeing you again, or it may set its little bell ringing. Your bird's trust will grow rapidly if it is allowed to fly outside the cage regularly and finds out that you are always there to help it out of a tight spot if necessary.

The Bird Is Joined by a Partner

Perhaps you were planning all along to get a companion for your parakeet and were just waiting for the first bird to become tame before getting the second one. Or perhaps you have begun to realize that you can't properly fill the role of surrogate partner for your parakeet. If you take some care in introducing the second parakeet, you will soon have a pair of birds that trust you and enjoy the contact with you but don't expect you to spend too much time with them because they keep busy with each other.

Try to find a breeder who will call you the day a young parakeet has left the nesting box. As already mentioned, the gender of the bird is of no great consequence. If two birds are of the same sex, one of them will adopt the role of the opposite sex. You should pick up the bird from the breeder no later than one day after the call. House it in a different room from the one your first parakeet is in. At this point the fledgling parakeet has had no experience with humans and is not afraid of them. It still likes to be held loosely in the hand and even settles down in it comfortably because the hand is reminiscent of the warmth of its nestling siblings. If your particular parakeet enjoys this, hold it in your hand as much as you can and talk softly to it. This way it will become used to you and your voice.

Crack some seeds from the birdseed mixture with a rock and spread them on the floor. Then put the bird down gently and see how much it eats. If it doesn't seem to you to eat enough, offer from your hand some zwieback crumbs, white bread softened in milk, or non-fat cottage cheese mixed with hard-boiled egg yolk. See if the young bird is already able to eat spray millet. At the same time keep giving it crushed seeds on the floor every two hours. It is important to offer the seeds on the floor because parakeets are programmed by nature to look for food on the ground.

After two or three days, set the young bird down on the floor where the older parakeet can see it and watch what happens. At first the older bird will be motionless with amazement, but then it will fly to the floor and circle the new arrival with great curiosity. Perhaps some parental instinct will be stirred, and it will start feeding the young bird. Or the latter may beg from the adult bird and will be fed by it. Just observe, and interfere only if the older bird starts chasing or biting the fledgling. If that happens, you will have to return the little one to its cage and try again the next day. Often an established bird will respond aggressively to a fellow parakeet out of jealousy. The first time I showed Mini to Manky I made the mistake of holding young Mini in my hand. Manky promptly ran up to Mini and pulled a feather from her head. When I placed her in front of him on the floor the next day, however, he started feeding her lovingly. They later made a perfect pair.

Questions About Free Flying

A parakeet that spends all its time in a small cage and is never allowed to fly free is a pitiful creature. The air is a bird's true element. In the wild, parakeets fly to foraging grounds, to watering places, and to escape enemies. Birds spend hours every day preening themselves in order to keep up their flying skills, for otherwise their lives would be in constant danger. A pet parakeet, too, has to be allowed to fly if it is to stay healthy.

Grooming of the plumage is essential for fast flying.

Should a Parakeet Be Allowed to Fly Free Only at Set Times?

A parakeet becomes thoroughly acquainted with its new surroundings only if it is allowed to fly around frequently and for a long period of time. Flying free not only increases the bird's comfort in its new world but also keeps it healthy. Since parakeets are by nature skillful flyers, I advocate letting them fly free all day in an absolutely "bird-proof" room (see page 41). A climbing tree or a hanging perch helps the birds take off and land without problems outside the cage. Place the tree or perch as far as you can from the cage where the food is, thus making the birds fly back and forth every time they want to eat or drink. Pairs of birds also continually motivate each other to fly around. If your birds can't fly free without your presence because, perhaps, the room isn't bird-proof, you should see to it that they have several sufficiently extended flying sessions a day.

How Do You Get the Bird to Return to Its Cage?

If your bird is hand-tame, you can carry it to the cage on your hand and hold it in front of the door in such a way that it is forced to enter. With a bird that is still afraid of your hand, hold the cage up to it in a position that makes it easy for the bird to step in. If nothing works, let the bird spend the night on its perch and don't worry. When it gets hungry and thirsty in the morning it will manage to find its way to the cage. Don't ever try to drive the bird from its chosen spot to the cage by waving a broom at it. Such a shocking experience would turn you into an enemy in the bird's eyes, an enemy to get away from.

Is There a Danger That the Bird Will Crash into a Window?

This is a danger only if the bird is not yet sufficiently acquainted with "its" room. Windows without curtains are particularly dangerous, for parakeets don't realize that the transparent glass is solid, and they can break their necks or sustain other serious injuries if they fly against a window. To help the bird recognize the window as a barrier, lower a shade all but 8 inches (20 cm) and turn the lights on in the room before letting the bird fly free the first time. This allows the bird to become safely acquainted with the room and all the objects in it. Then raise the shade a couple of inches every day until your bird has learned to respect the window as an invisible wall. This generally takes only a few days, and the lesson will probably carry over to windows in other rooms. There is not so much danger of a parakeet flying into a mirror because birds stop their flight in time when confronted with their own image in a mirror.

Why Does a Parakeet Flap Its Wings Without Flying?

Very young birds still unable to fly exercise their flight muscles by flapping their wings. Sometimes they hold on with the bill to a branch or a cage bar when doing this. Breeders can tell by this behavior that the young birds are getting ready to leave the nest box. Adult birds suffering from lack of exercise also flap their wings, trying to counter their enforced inactivity.

What children ask: "Could my parakeet strangle itself on the mobile if we let it fly free in the room?" (Question from a 12-year-old girl.) The parakeet might try to hold onto a mobile to swing on it or to nibble on it. In doing so, it might indeed strangle itself. The mobile should therefore be removed from the room where the bird is allowed to fly.

Parakeets have trouble orienting themselves in complete dark and may crash against walls and furniture or flutter wildly in the cage if a noise startles them at night. They can easily injure themselves that way. Leaving a small light on helps them recognize where they are.

Life With Your Parakeet

Once your parakeet begins to feel at home, it will try more and more confidently to satisfy its curiosity, its need for activity, and its desire for companionship. If the bird feels comfortable in its cage, this will at first be its place of safety and refuge. But once it has explored the room and discovered safe landing places, it will start spending more time there. Timidly at first, but gradually more and more self-confidently, it will begin to test everything with its beak, nibbling, shoving, and sending objects tumbling to the floor. If there is a bird tree in the room, this will probably become the bird's favorite hangout. After all, the tree is decorated with a mirror, a bell, and tassles of hemp rope.

Taking Charge of the New Environment

In the room there are many small objects that fascinate a parakeet. Thus Maxi, the piano player, loved a small ivory elephant better than any toy designed for parakeets. This elephant was the smallest of a row of elephants displayed on a shelf and measured less than an inch. First Maxi tried to knock each of the elephants over, but he succeeded only with the smallest one. This one he could carry off in his beak. He knocked it to the floor, then picked it up by the trunk, and marched through the room proudly carrying his booty. Finally he flew to his cage, still carrying the elephant. Now, however, a problem arose. The elephant was to sleep next to Maxi perched on the swing, but it kept falling down. Eventually Maxi solved the problem by changing his sleeping place to a perch next to the food cup, with the elephant sleeping in the cup.

A parakeet owner wrote the following to me about her bird's favorite occupation: "In our dining area there is a shelf with liqueur glasses that have little covers that flip up. Our parakeet Pepi would raise the covers one after the other and then close them again. His greatest pleasure was to perch on that shelf, look down, and follow everything that was going on below. Below the shelf hung a mobile made up of small hearts. Pepi would sit below the mobile for hours letting the hearts stroke his head as they moved. If I failed to put the glasses back in their proper places after cleaning the shelf, Pepi would

There is only one perch on this colorful little cart, and it is promptly claimed by the self-assured female.

Parakeets love some toys with a passion and are heartbroken when the beloved object breaks. It is therefore a good idea to have several of the same items in reserve. If you have a pair of birds, you should always give them two identical toys to prevent squabbles.

...except for the head.

Parakeets can reach all parts of the body with their bill...

knock them all down and not be satisfied until I arranged them correctly."

Games Make for Physical Activity

Pet parakeets are often bored, especially if a bird is kept singly and thus lacks the stimulation of a partner.

The day can sometimes drag on even for a pair of birds since, as pet birds, they never have to go in search of food, which is usually provided in abundance. They rarely, if ever, have to attend to parental duties. There is no need to look for a nesting cavity or to assert themselves against neighbors, and only rarely does an occasion arise when a partner or a nesting site has to be defended against rivals. Because of the rather monotonous tenor of life, parakeets should have plenty of objects to nibble on and play with and receive lots of affection and stimulation from their keeper.

Happy, healthy parakeets like playing as much as small children do. Any accessible object is examined to see if it can provide work for the beak—often with considerable success. A sheet of letter paper on your desk will soon be decorated with a zigzag edge, a poster on the wall will first be used as a perch and later reduced to confetti. Wallpaper and books may suffer similar treatment.

Parakeets also delight in balancing on a pen or pencil in the hand of "their" person, and they love to get at that thing inside that leaves the strange marks on the paper. The writing ends of pens and pencils exert a magic attraction on the birds, as does anything that glitters, shines, reflects, turns, or can be moved. You have no idea how much useful play material your parakeet will discover in your living quarters. But for the bird's own good and for the appearance of your possessions it is better to get a few ordinary toys at the beginning, things that are easy to find and present no danger to the bird. Make sure that all chains and strings from which toys are hung are heavy and short enough that a bird cannot conceivably choke itself on them.

A brass bell hanging near the sleeping spot often becomes a beloved companion for a parakeet that is kept singly. The fleeting reflection the bird glimpses of itself in the metal is perceived as a fellow bird. It provides consolation during lonely spells and is treated sometimes as partner, at other times as a rival. And the sound of the bell reinforces the bird's own vocal expression of all kinds of moods.

If there is a pair of parakeets, the male often uses the bell to indicate his mood. If he yanks on the chain violently, this is meant to show the female what a brave fellow she has for a partner; and if he swings the bell high, making it ring, this is meant to prove his potency.

The mirror fulfills similar functions, but here the bird's reflection shows more clearly and is less fleeting and can therefore serve as a steady partner. A male will feed the mirror image if no female is present, and a female will do the same in the absence of chicks.

The mirror doesn't always play the same role. Sometimes it is perceived as an enemy that has to be fought or as a partner that is not behaving properly. Some authorities claim that mirrors are harmful for birds because they stimulate sexual feelings. But If no mirror is present, a lone male parakeet will turn to other objects to woo and get excited by. If there is harm in this it is not caused by the mirror but by the unnatural situation of a bird living alone, without others of its own kind.

A rope of hemp or cotton hanging from the roof of the cage or the bird tree is used by many parakeets for performing and inventing ever new climbing tricks. But the rope should not be too long or too thin so that there is no possibility of the bird strangling itself on it. As an added precaution and to facilitate climbing, you can tie a few knots in the rope. If two birds fight over the rope, it is best to supply a second one.

Plastic balls sold at pet stores and designed

Birds groom the underside of the wings very carefully.

Grooming takes up several hours a day. Of course, a bird doesn't groom itself for hours at a time, but works at it in bits and pieces, usually between periods of rest and activity.

especially for parakeets are loved by these birds. These balls are actually round cages with a small bell inside and light enough for the birds to pick up with the bill and carry or throw some distance. They are ideal for solitary playing and for games with you, and they, too, quite often become surrogates for a sexual partner. My parakeet Manky always had such a ball. Within a few weeks the ball would disintegrate and Manky would go into mourning. I would offer him several new ones of the same color, but they would be ignored for days until he gradually formed a new attachment to one of them.

A small spinning top, made of wood or plastic, about the size of a hazelnut and without sharp edges, is also fascinating to parakeets. They watch spellbound while the top spins and dances, not daring to approach. But once the speed slows and the top begins to wobble, they usually run up to it and shove it with the beak, effectively stopping it. Expectant looks in your direction will urge you to repeat the magic show.

Tossing things to the floor is another favorite sport. The parakeet doesn't care in the least what is sent sailing over the edge. What matters is that it, the bird, has made the object fall and can watch it. Anything round on the table—like a marble—will do but usually rolls off too fast for the bird to witness the downward plunge. That's why small wooden or plastic toy cars are more satisfying. First the car has to be rolled in the right direction with the beak—which requires some practice—and then it has to be released at the right moment if the bird is to get a good view of the tumble. If you have a toy car and a few marbles, you will become an ideal playmate for your bird, and you will be amazed at how many variations of the basic game it will invent.

Little Treats

The saying "The way to a man's heart is through his stomach" applies to parakeets as well. If you offer your parakeet spray millet from your hand, the bird is likely to forget its fear of the human hand and jump up on your finger in order to get at the treat. Fruit may also tempt the bird. It will pick the seeds off a strawberry with relish or drink the juice of a cherry that is cut in half and held up.

Someone to Play With

Many of the toys you can buy for your parakeet become interesting only if you help your bird play with them. Anything round and not heavy enough to hurt in case of a collision can be used for a racing competition. Parakeets like best running after a rolling object. If the object comes at them head-on, they often react with a mixture of fear and aggressiveness. Whether the bird will run away or deflect the object with its beak depends on how familiar it is with the approaching thing. Here, too, you will be amazed at your bird's inventiveness. Thus Manky, whom I have already mentioned repeatedly, made up a game to play with a small plastic ruler. As soon as he saw the ruler he would hop onto it and squat down. That was a signal for me to push the plastic ball across the table with the ruler while he hung on and tried to pick up the ball with his beak.

Petch, my cousin's parakeet, loved playing with a ball of crumpled up aluminum foil. He would hold onto it with both feet and then roll on his back, holding the ball up. I was now to try to get the ball away from him, but he held on so tightly that I usually lifted the bird up along with the foil. If I swung bird and foil up in the air, he would fly in a wide arc back to the table and catch hold of the rolling ball, ready to start the game all over.

Affection and Talk

For a parakeet, being close to you and listening to you is almost as satisfying as playing. You should take a few minutes several times a day to talk to your parakeet. This creates a feeling of closeness and reassures the bird that it is not alone but belongs to you. It will love sitting on your hand and listening to the words it already knows. And during these intimate moments it will also learn new words.

Manky was so eager to listen to my words and songs that it almost amounted to an addiction. Several times a day he would come up to me, clearly urging me to "perform." Unfortunately, I didn't always have time. So I recorded his repertoire on a tape and played it for him every so often. Manky would literally lie on the small speaker and listen with complete concentration. He knew the entire routine by heart, and if I paused a little too long, he would impatiently continue the text himself without ever missing a word.

Here is another report from a parakeet owner showing how much birds enjoy listening to the human voice: "Pepi loved to hear the bedside story I read every evening to my young daughter. As soon as he heard her brushing her teeth, he would fly impatiently to the bathroom. While I read he sat on her shoulder, listened attentively, and occasionally added some chatter of his own."

Grooming a guinea pig's mane is a lot of work. In return the guinea pig may let the bird take a bite of its lettuce.

Rest Periods Are Essential

No parakeet is active ceaselessly from morning until night. Birds rest several times during the day. They may actually sleep, or they may assume their sleeping position and mutter their entire repertoire of sounds to themselves. Sometimes you can understand clearly what a bird is saying, and sometimes what you hear is a garbled mixture of words and nonsense syllables. If a parakeet sits near a window, it may like to look out peacefully for some time. Or it may sit quietly next to its mirror or plastic companion.

Every Feather Is Groomed

Parakeets also spend many hours a day preening their plumage. One after the other, each feather is pulled through the beak. Dust is removed, and the feather is smoothed and oiled. For the feathers of the body, oil is picked up with an agile motion of the beak from a gland low on the back, just above the tail. The feathers of the head are rubbed directly over the gland. Parakeets can turn their heads 180 degrees, and by twisting the head up and down, they can reach even the lower abdomen and the vent. The long tail and wing feathers are carefully drawn through the beak their entire length, which requires acrobatic twists and turns of the body.

The thin layer of fat covering the plumage acts as a water repellent. It keeps birds from getting drenched in the rain and thus unable to fly—a state of great peril to parakeets living in the wild.

Attention to Hygiene Is a Must

Like all pets, parakeets create some dirt. Even outside the molting season some down feathers will float in the air. Every time a bird shakes its plumage, it creates a small dust cloud. Bits of food and, especially, empty husks of birdseed will whirl up into the air when the bird flaps its wings, and they don't all come to rest again in the cage. In addition, the birds produce small droppings every 12 to 15 minutes wherever they happen to sit. Most of the dirt can be quickly removed with a vacuum cleaner, and even the droppings hardly ever leave a mark. But it is important to clean the cage, the bird tree or hanging perch, and all the various objects the bird plays with regularly (see How-to: Maintenance, page 58).

Vacations

If you like to go away for a vacation you have to plan ahead, not only for your own accommodations, but also for those of your bird.

Going abroad with your bird is not a good idea because your bird will most likely be quarantined—if not when you leave the country, then when you return.

A car trip is possible, but if you travel in the summer you have to avoid extreme heat and also drafts. Parakeets can get sick and die if they are exposed to drafts. In a hotel or motel room your bird has to stay locked in its cage because cleaning personnel don't worry about open doors and windows or about drafts when they do your room. A tent is not an option if you vacation with a bird, but renting a cottage or other living quarters is a possibility.

It's nice to take sips of water running from the faucet.

But taking a bath in the hand of a trusted human...

...is even nicer.

Staying home in its familiar surroundings is certainly preferable from the bird's point of view. But you will have to find a reliable caretaker for your parakeet, someone who will come in at least twice a day to feed it, play and talk with it, and let it fly free in the room. It would be ideal, of course, if the caretaker could move into your apartment or house for the time you are away.

Friends or relatives may take the bird while you are away if you trust them and know that the bird will be welcome there. Write down instructions, including what the bird likes to eat, the things in the daily schedule that mean a lot to it, and perhaps the things it is afraid of. Send along all the various items the bird needs as well as the food that forms its basic staple, and make sure that it will be allowed to fly free a lot in its home away from home.

Pet stores will often board parakeets for a small charge. There the bird will probably be well taken care of, but it won't be able to fly free. This deprivation will be partially made up for by the voices of other birds at the pet store.

In case of illness, and especially if you plan ahead for a stay in the hospital, I recommend any of the last three alternatives. For the eventuality that you might have to go to the hospital unexpectedly without being able to

go home first, I suggest that you always leave the bird with a good supply of birdseed. In an emergency, you can give the police the key to your apartment. They will pick up the bird and take it where you tell them to leave it.

Advice for "single parents": If you live alone with your parakeet you should scout for a reliable caretaker before the need for one arises. Animal shelters often have addresses of bird lovers willing to take in a bird or two in an emergency or during vacation. Try to arrange a meeting with the person so that you can contact him or her quickly in case of need and will know that your parakeet is in good hands.

How-to: Maintenance

A parakeet devotes several hours a day to preening. It smoothes all its feathers with its beak, frees them of dust and dirt, and greases them with a secretion from the uropygial gland (see Glossary).

Schedule of Chores
Photos 1, 2, 3, and 5
Cleaning all utensils the bird comes in contact with and some other precautionary and hygienic measures you have to take are just as important as the bird's own efforts at keeping its plumage immaculate.

Daily Chores
• All perches should be scrubbed with a small metal brush that removes all traces of feces. Dry the perches off with a damp paper towel.
• Remove any dirt from the sand in the drawer at the bottom of the cage and from the tub in which the bird tree stands. Use a spoon for this. If necessary, add fresh sand.
   Important: When you take out the sand drawer, place something of appropriate size in front of the opening so that the bird cannot slip out through it.
• Wash food dishes and water dispenser with hot water in the morning (see Photos 1–3), dry them, and refill them. (The leftover birdseed can be used again once all the empty husks are removed.)
• Skim off empty seed husks again in the afternoon with a spoon—don't blow them off, this stirs up too much dust—and refill the dish so that the birds will have food when they wake up the next morning.

Weekly Chores
• Wash bottom tray and sand drawer well with warm water and dry. Supply fresh sand.
• Throw out birdseed left in cup. Wash all food dishes with hot water, dry, and fill with fresh food.
• Wash the perches of the cage and the bird tree with hot water after scrubbing them with a metal brush (see Photo 5) and dry them.
• Remove toys, wash in warm water, and dry them.

Monthly Chores
• Remove bottom tray and sand drawer and place them, along with the cage top, in the bathtub. Hose off with warm water and scrub well with a brush. Then rub everything dry.
• Replace branches that have been gnawed with new ones that have been washed with hot water and dried off.
• Clean the branches and toys of the bird tree thoroughly as described above. Replace a generous amount of sand. If the bird tree incorporates plants, carefully remove traces of droppings on the leaves with water.
   Important: Don't use soaps, rinses, or other chemicals for this cleaning; they might be harmful

1. Scrub and dry the bath house after every use.

2. Water dispenser and food dishes have to be washed every day in warm water.

3. Dishwashing brushes and bottle brushes work well for this.

4. Some parakeets don't take full baths but like to moisten their plumage on wet leaves.

to the bird. Clean, hot water does the job. Cages with bars that are not coated with epoxy resin should not be washed but only wiped clean with a damp cloth.

Tip: Fresh droppings on smooth surfaces are easily removed with a paper towel; if they land on textiles, let them dry and then vacuum or brush them off.

Fun with Water
Photo 4

If you catch your parakeet trying desperately to dip its abdomen into its water cup, this is a clear sign that the bird would like to bathe. Many parakeets enjoy frequent and lengthy baths; others avoid water and only dampen their feathers now and then on some wet greens. Find out what your bird's inclinations are. Here are some possibilities:

A full bath: A bath house that is hung into the door opening of the cage serves well for this purpose. The bird can dip its tail and belly feathers into the water, but because of the limited space it cannot really get its wings wet.

• An alternative: Use a flower pot saucer made of clay (diameter about 10 inches [26 cm]). This is big enough for the bird to be able to spread out one wing at a time in the water.

• Preparation: Pour about ¾ inch (2 cm) lukewarm water into the bath house or saucer. Hang the bath house into the cage opening when the bird is in the cage. Or set the saucer on a

table. Then it is up to the bird whether or not and how it will satisfy its need for bathing.

• Reaction: At first the bird will probably taste the water, then fluff up its feathers and dance excitedly around the saucer before deciding whether to play and splash in it or to forego the adventure. Even if the decision is negative you should keep offering the opportunity of a bath. Once it overcomes its first fear of water, the bird itself will let you know when it is in the mood for a bath, perhaps by tapping its beak against a water glass or by trying once again to dive into its water dish.

A shower bath: If the fear of water proves stronger than the desire to bathe when a full bath is offered, you can try administering a gentle, lukewarm shower with a plant mister held at a little distance. After the first surprise the bird may well accept this compromise happily. Just make sure that the plant mister has never been used for spraying liquid plant fertilizer or pesticides.

A dew bath: If your bird refuses even to take such a shower bath, place some wet greens on the cage roof. It may enjoy wetting its feathers on the leaves.

You can also bring in some damp herbs, dandelion greens, or young tree leaves from your garden and offer them in the flower pot saucer. In their native Australia, parakeets habitually take dew baths in the morning (see Photo 4).

5. Scrub droppings with wire brush, rub branch clean with damp cloth.

Questions About Taming Birds and

Every parakeet owner wants a tame bird, preferably one that talks and says the right thing at the right time. How tame a bird becomes depends on how close it feels to its keeper. The more you play and talk with your bird, the friendlier and more affectionate it will become. But not all parakeets are interested in talking, and you can't make a bird talk. Only if a bird starts to babble on its own does it make sense to encourage it by saying things over and over for it to imitate.

A fellow bird, also a male.

How Long Does It Take for a Parakeet to Become Tame?

If your parakeet is not over three months when you get it, chances are good that it will turn into a friendly and tame bird. Considerably older parakeets that are not used to people only rarely become hand-tame. But if they are treated with sensitivity, they may get accustomed to having people around and overcome their worst fear of them. Whatever the case, the degree of success depends on your patience and persistence and on the temperament of your particular bird. The more time you spend with the bird, the faster it will become tame. But there is no sure-fire "recipe" for taming parakeets because different birds respond to different approaches. Some can't resist treats like spray millet, some respond to games, others like to be stroked gently or love simply to sit close to you and listen to your voice.

How Can a Second Parakeet Be Hand-tamed?

A second parakeet—preferably a very young bird—should not initially be kept in the same room with the first one. You should spend a lot of time with it until it, too, has become hand-tame. If you let it join the older bird immediately, it will be completely absorbed by the latter and remain shy of you. However, in time it will learn that you are not dangerous, that you bring food, and that you help it out of tight spots. Then it will gradually become less shy and eventually accept you as completely as the first bird does.

Teaching Them to Talk

How Do You Teach a Parakeet to Talk? Do Only Males Talk?

Parakeets with a talent for speaking will repeat many of the words and phrases they hear a lot, such as greetings and names. But you can also teach your parakeet deliberately. Keep saying the same word or phrase in recurring situations: for instance, "Good morning" when you first come into the bird's room in the morning, or "Look, a treat" when you bring food. If the bird is looking expectantly at you, respond with a phrase, always pronounced in the same way. Go over the bird's entire repertoire during the times devoted to close togetherness. If none of this produces any results, it is because your bird is not interested in talking. If a parakeet has lived alone for a long time or exclusively with other birds, it is not likely to start talking now.

More male parakeets learn to talk than females, but I also know a number of females with quite impressive vocabularies.

Is Talking Bad for the Birds?

Parakeets that talk are birds that are at ease and relaxed. They have close contact with one or several humans whom they regard as members of their flock, and they have chosen to utilize their inborn ability to modulate sounds to imitate human speech for the purpose of communicating with their human flock members. Talking is no more harmful than the prattling and screeching parakeets do naturally.

What children ask: "Can a parakeet that knows how to talk read too?" (Question from an eight-year-old girl.)
No, parakeets can't read. That's because their brains are different from ours. But they have a different way of "reading" from ours. They can "read" the signs of nature, understand the gestures and utterances of other parakeets, and sense our moods.

It is a bad sign if a parakeet that used to talk stops either suddenly or gradually. Senility may be the cause, or the beginning of a disease. Watch the bird closely and, if possible, take it to the vet for examination.

The Proper
Diet

In their native Australia, parakeets feed primarily on the seeds of various grasses and other plants. When they range over arid areas in their search for food, they stop wherever there is any water because they need to drink to soften the dry kernels in their crops. If all the streams and puddles have dried up, the birds drink the dew clinging to the grass when they forage in the savanna first thing in the morning. It has been shown that in the course of foraging, parakeets also absorb small amounts of mineral-rich sand and tiny stones that assist digestion.

The Basic Staple

What we have learned of the feeding habits of parakeets in the wild enables us to offer our pet birds a well-balanced mixture of dry seeds. Depending on the manufacturer, commercial parakeet seed mixtures are composed of about 30 percent canary grass seed, 25 percent white millet, 20 percent yellow millet, 15 percent oats and groats and red millet, 5 percent niger seed, and 5 percent linseed. High-quality mixtures also contain some thistle, anise, rape, sesame, and safflower seed.

Some also include vitamin pellets with iodine that is supposed to prevent thyroid problems.

Be Careful When Buying Birdseed

When buying birdseed for your parakeet, look not only for the packing date but also examine the condition of the package itself. In pet stores, supermarkets, garden centers, and drug stores I have repeatedly found packages with expiration dates more than 18 months past. On some there was a printed notice: "Freshness guaranteed for 18 months after packing. See date on bottom," but no date was stamped on the bottom. Other packages were stamped "May be sold until..." but without any date.

Dealers don't automatically take outdated merchandise off their shelves. You as the consumer must protect your own interests. If a package is dented or torn, chances are that the contents are no longer in prime condition. Even birdseed from an undamaged package may be spoiled and may make your bird sick. The seed may be rotten, moldy, or contain vermin. This is how you can tell:

• Rotten seeds have a penetrating odor;

Leaves and blossoms from a fresh fruit tree branch taste especially good. This is something you can treat your bird to as often as you like.

healthy seeds have no smell.

• Mold shows up as a whitish-gray film on the seeds. You have to look very closely, though. Run some seeds across your hand a few at a time, and spot check with a magnifying glass.

• In the case of vermin, some seeds are clumped together and fine filaments resembling spider's webs run through the birdseed.

Proper storage: If you have only one or two parakeets, one package of birdseed will last several weeks. But if you have more birds, you will probably want to mix your own seeds bought at a seed store. In this case you will have to store the birdseed for a longer period. To prevent spoilage, keep the seeds in a dry, dark, but airy space. Hang them in an appropriate room in cloth bags made of natural fiber. Mice and other pests can't get at the seeds as easily if the seeds hang in bags as if they are stored on shelves.

Wrong storage: Seeds in plastic bags, tightly closed tin or plastic containers or canning jars tend to spoil because not enough air gets at them, and their nutritional value decreases rapidly if they are exposed to light.

A parakeet will pass up anything for the sake of spray millet.

How Much Food Do the Birds Need?

• Put two teaspoonfuls of birdseed per bird in the food dishes. If there are two dishes, put two teaspoonfuls in each because the bird will have trouble reaching the seeds if they are too low in the dish.

• Skim off empty husks with a spoon in the afternoon, otherwise the bird can't get at the seeds underneath.

My advice: Don't try to blow the empty husks off. If you blow them off indoors they are all over the room, and if you do it by an open window the bird might escape.

• If there is only a little bit of birdseed left in the afternoon, add another teaspoonful. There should be plenty of food for the bird to eat before it goes to sleep and when it wakes up in the morning.

Do always give your bird plenty of food. Parakeets that are properly kept eat only as much as they need. And you might sometime be prevented from getting home on time, in which case well filled food dishes prove a blessing.

Do not try to keep a bird from getting fat by rationing its birdseed. Birds have a very active metabolism and need to eat small portions frequently during the day. Parakeets become obese primarily if they are not able to fly enough or if they lack stimulation to keep busy and are then fed unnecessary, fattening treats to relieve their boredom. Bird treats are sold in the shape of little bars and hearts to which seeds are stuck with a sugar or honey glaze.

Viable Seeds Have Full Nutritional Value

Reputable manufacturers conform to the practice of indicating the packing date of their products, but this in itself is of no great value because there is no way of knowing how old the seed was when it was packaged. Seeds are harvested once a year. Stored under proper conditions, they remain viable for one year and are fit for consumption for a second year. Since nutritional value gradually declines even under proper storage, however, only seeds that can still germinate are a truly fit food for cage birds. That is why you should spot check the seeds' viability for every package you buy. If the seeds germinate, they are rich in vitamins and nutrients; if only about half sprout, you should throw out the package and buy another (see Sprouting Recipe, page 69). Associations of cage bird fanciers are now requesting that manufacturers of animal feeds indicate the expiration date rather than the packing date on their products.

Only viable seeds are rich in vitamins that keep your parakeet healthy. If you don't pay enough attention to viability, you run the risk of deficiency disease in your birds.

Don't Forget the Drinking Water

Of course parakeets need fresh drinking water every day. Tap water that is not too cold will do. Or you can buy a special, commercial bird drink. Best of all is uncarbonated mineral water because of the minerals in it. Weakly brewed black tea or herb tea should be given only to sick birds and only if the vet recommends it.

Important: If you are not using an automatic water dispenser you should replace the drinking water in the course of the day because it will get fouled by droppings and seed husks.

In a harmonious relationship, the male knows exactly what his mate likes best.

Fresh Foods: A Welcome Change

Fresh foods include mixed raw vegetables, fruits, and herbs. Caged birds can never get too much of these because the basic birdseed mixtures don't contain all the vitamins birds need to stay healthy, maintain their plumage in good condition, and keep from becoming too fat. Fresh food also provides work for the beak—healthy activity that keeps birds from eating out of boredom. That is why you should give your parakeet fresh fruit and vegetables of the season every day, preferably freshly bought at a farmer's market—anything you use for yourself and your family. But please take note of the things that don't agree with parakeets.

Suitable raw vegetables: Eggplant, endive, green peas and their shells, small amounts of fennel and cucumber, young dandelion greens, sweet corn at the milky stage, beet greens, carrots, unsprayed lettuce, green peppers, sorrel, spinach leaves, tomatoes, zucchini.

Suitable raw fruit: Pineapples, apples, apricots, bananas, pears, blackberries, strawberries, figs, raspberries, cherries, kiwi fruit, tangerines, melons, oranges, peaches, and grapes.

Bad for birds: All members of the cabbage family, raw and green potatoes, green beans, lettuce that has been sprayed with pesticides, grapefruit, rhubarb, plums, lemons, avocados.

Important: Never feed the bird anything directly from the refrigerator. Everything should be at room temperature, have been washed and dabbed dry, and peeled if appropriate. Cut out rotten spots and don't be stingy about it. Anything with mold on it has to be thrown out because mold can penetrate into the interior in invisible form.

How Do You Offer Fresh Foods?

Fruits and vegetables with a firm consistency, such as pineapples, apples, pears, carrots, and zucchini, should be cut into sections or slices big enough to be stuck between the cage bars. Softer fruits are cut into small cubes, mixed with grated vegetables, and offered in a small bowl. Don't give up if your parakeet at first refuses to touch fresh food. At some point curiosity will prove too strong, and the bird will poke at the food with the beak. Once some of the fruit juice reaches the taste buds, the barrier is broken, but this can take days or even weeks. Don't get discouraged in the meantime. Keep offering fresh food every day.

Parakeets that have learned to accept fresh food love putting their beaks to work on it. They break off small pieces of firm fruit, grind up each bite in the beak, and then let it drop to the floor. With soft, juicy fruit they absorb primarily the juice. Even if they seem to just play with the food, some bits of fruit are swallowed, enough to supply necessary vitamins and minerals. If you keep in mind how little a parakeet weighs, you realize that the birds need much smaller quantities of these substances than we do.

Parakeets belong to the parrot family, but their beaks are not as strong as those of their larger relatives. Nor are they able, like parrots, to hold the food with their toes. Parakeets are very skillful at shelling seeds with their beak and small, thick tongue, and they can take bites of soft fruit. Harder fruit has to be grated for them, or offered in thick slices on which they can gnaw. Many parakeets love to pick the little seeds off strawberries, but they can do so only if someone holds the berries for them. They can eat cherries and grapes only if these are cut in half. If you hold these halved fruits for them, many parakeets enjoy drinking the juice.

Ways to Try to Convert Birds to Fresh Food

From the letters I receive from readers I know that many parakeet owners worry because their birds refuse—and have refused for years—to touch fruit and vegetables. There are some little tricks that may prove helpful. Most parakeets are very eager to taste the food we humans eat. Try placing a small amount of fruit and vegetables on a plate and sit down with the food when your bird is around. When you start eating, the parakeet may want to join you. After a few days you may no longer have to share your meals with the bird because it has learned to enjoy fresh food. If you know someone who has a parakeet that loves fresh food, invite this bird to your house. Whether the two parakeets meet in adjacent cages or are allowed to range freely in the room, they are bound to be interested in each other and will watch each other with an eagle eye. Serve the birds some fresh food after a while. I'd be willing to bet that your bird will soon imitate the stranger and start eating too.

Herbs and Wild Plants

Herbs and wild plants are a good addition to the diet if they resemble plants parakeets eat in the wild.

From your kitchen and garden: Basil, borage, fennel, chervil, bee balm, mint, and parsley are good additions to the menu.

From fields and meadows (unfertilized) or along country roads (but not along highways because of car exhaust fumes) you can collect wild plants. Parakeets are fond of the half-ripe seeds of annual bluegrass and wild red millet and of the leaves and flowers of cow vetch. They also like the flowers of daisies without stems, open seed capsules of wild pansies, the flowers and fruits of hawthorn, and the leaves and stems of young dandelion plants. Sorrel, shepherd's purse, chickweed, and watercress are also welcome.

Offer these plants held to the cage roof with a clothespin after rinsing them well under lukewarm water and shaking them dry.

Minerals and Trace Elements

Parakeets, like humans, need minerals and trace elements in their diet, but in minute quantities. Seeds and fresh foods contain these on a microscopic but adequate scale. The most important of these substances, calcium and phosphorus, are always plentiful in mineral blocks, cuttlebone, and in the bird sand. Make sure you always have an extra mineral block or cuttlebone on hand because often a bird that has spurned them for weeks will suddenly develop a craving and gnaw a stone or cuttlebone down to nothing in a few hours.

Important: Don't offer cuttlebones, which the birds use for whetting the beak on just like mineral blocks, to females during the reproductive cycle, because some hens react by developing egg binding (see Glossary).

Dinner Is Served!

In addition to a mixture of dry, viable seeds a parakeet's diet has to include fresh foods—vegetables, fruit, and greens. These have to be supplied to satisfy the bird's daily vitamin and mineral requirements. The fresh food has to be served at room temperature, not straight from the refrigerator. Calcium and phosphorus are also contained in the mineral block, the cuttlebone, and the birdsand. Fresh drinking water every day is also essential.

Other Things the Birds Like

Pet stores sell various other foods parakeets enjoy. Or you can prepare special treats yourself.

What you can buy:

• Spray millet is the most important addition to a parakeet's basic daily diet. A highly nutritious, natural food, spray millet is ideal for breeding pairs, youngsters, as well as weak and sick birds. Healthy, adult parakeets, however, should be given no more than about 2 inches (6 cm) a day, or they will stop eating other food, which makes for too one-sided a diet. Attach the millet to the cage with a clothespin or a special millet spray holder.

• Supplemental seeds, packaged in small quantities, are sold with various claims of their benefits. There are some that are supposed to help birds during the molt and no doubt contain vitamins and other health-promoting substances, though no nutritional analysis is given. Others, like the so-called "talk pearls," are unlikely to produce the promised benefits. A parakeet's aptitude for talking, if present, is innate, and you have to develop it by diligently repeating the phrases you want the bird to learn (see page 55).

• Little hearts, rings, and sticks covered with seeds are sold as special treats. Nobody knows whether parakeets really like the taste

Fresh water. But how do I get at it?

or chew on them simply to satisfy their need for gnawing. The seeds are stuck to the forms with a sugar or honey glaze, which contains unneeded calories. Fresh branches are much healthier to gnaw on and supply the birds with valuable substances present beneath the bark (see How-to: The Cage, pages 34 and 35).

• I do, however, consider vitamin supplements a beneficial addition to a bird's diet because there is no way of accurately ascertaining the vitamin content of birdseed or of fruit and vegetables. Vitamins are crucial to health. The smaller the organism, the more sensitive it is to vitamin deficiencies. You can buy vitamin supplements suitable for parakeets at pet stores or drug stores. The vitamins can be added to the drinking water, to the fresh food, or sprinkled over sprouts. Always check the expiration date; old vitamins are worthless.

What you can prepare yourself:

• Hard-boiled egg yolk mixed with a little nonfat cottage cheese supplies valuable proteins. A half a teaspoonful once a week will benefit your parakeet.

• Freshly cracked grains—which you may be using for your own breakfast cereal—can be given to your bird. Offer a little bit, soaked in lukewarm water, every day.

• You should give your birds sprouted seeds every day for a period of three to four weeks in mid-winter, in early spring, during molting, and when the birds raise young. An even better idea is to regularly alternate three-week periods of sprouts with four sproutless weeks.

A bird that doesn't eat any fresh food should get sprouted seeds all the time. Sprouts prevent nutritional deficiencies from developing, help weak birds gain strength, and keep healthy ones fit. You can use the basic birdseed mixture or oat and wheat kernels as well as other seed mixtures sold at health food stores for sprouting. As soon as viable seeds start to absorb water, chemical reactions take place inside them that trigger sprouting. In this process vitamins, minerals, and trace elements are released that increase the nutritional value of the swelling seeds, and even more of the actual sprouts.

Luckily I can fly.

What if I were to fall in? Better hold on tight while I drink.

A Sprouting Recipe

Very important: Don't cover the seeds airtight while they absorb water. If you do, they are likely to develop mold. The sprouts, too, mold quickly when they are removed from the container. That is why you have to throw out whatever the bird has not consumed after about two hours.

• Place ½ teaspoonful each of birdseed, oat kernels, wheat kernels, and, if you like, other seeds into a jar, cover them with ¾ inch (2 cm) water, and soak them, covered, for 24 hours.

• Rinse the seeds off with lukewarm water, drain off the water, place in a glass bowl, cover loosely with a plate, and let stand for 48 hours at room temperature and exposed to daylight.

• As soon as the tips of the sprouts show, you can give the seeds to the birds. Or, even better, wait until the sprouts are ⅜ to ¾ inch (1–2 cm) long. Rinse off again under lukewarm water, let the water drip off, and offer the sprouts to the bird in a small dish.

Nibbling at the Dining Table

Few people can resist the sight of a tame parakeet hopping from plate to plate, taking a bite here and a bite there. But being on the table, where there are hot dishes, strong spices, and other things that don't agree with birds, is not without risk. A bird can burn itself on hot food—one parakeet I knew was so eager that it jumped into a serving dish full of hot soup and promptly died—burn its tongue, or choke on spicy food. If in spite of these dangers you allow your parakeet on the table at mealtimes, you have to have some special tidbits ready for it. Foods good for birds are a bit of cooled potato, a few noodles, some mildly seasoned vegetables, a bite of white bread, or some fruit. If the parakeet is left in its cage in the same room where people are eating, it will soon begin to eat, too—from its own dish.

Ideal Foods for the First Days

During the first ten days or so in its new home a parakeet will enjoy the following daily menu:

• the birdseed mixture the bird is used to,
• unlimited amounts of spray millet,
• plenty of fresh water,
• a slice of apple and a big piece of banana in a dish,
• one or two slices of carrot or two teaspoonfuls of grated carrot (whichever the bird prefers),
• a small bunch of parsley or chickweed.

Questions Concerning Diet

We know that parakeets live mostly on grass seeds in the wild. When raising their young they need half-ripe seeds, which are nutritionally richer than dry ones. We can supply our cage birds with extra nutrients by giving them sprouted seeds, occasional high-protein foods, and lots of fruit and vegetables. The more varied the menu, the more healthful the diet of your parakeet.

How wonderful to have all the food you could possibly want!

How Often Should a Bird's Food Be Replenished?

Put about one tablespoonful of birdseed per bird into the dish. In the afternoon the empty husks have to be removed or the bird will not be able to get at the seeds underneath. Don't blow the husks off at an open window because the bird might escape. Instead, skim them off with a small spoon and add more seed if there is only a little left in the dish. A bird should never be left without birdseed even if it tends toward obesity because its body needs regular refueling. Fruit and vegetables should be offered twice a day fresh because fresh food loses its nutritional value when left at room temperature. Sprouted seeds, too, should be removed after a couple of hours, especially on hot days, because they spoil quickly and are then harmful to birds.

How Can You Get a Parakeet to Eat Fruit?

This may be difficult if the bird did not acquire the habit when it was young. But don't give up too quickly! Keep offering fruit, if necessary while playing with the bird. If a bird pecks at an apple or strawberry, it will probably like the taste. Often the presence of another parakeet that likes fruit and eats it with your bird watching helps. Or eat the fruit yourself in front of your parakeet. Perhaps the bird will get so curious that it will want a taste, too. If you tie a bunch of herbs still wet from washing to the cage roof, your bird may bite at the greens and decide it likes fresh herbs.

Why Does My Parakeet Dig Holes in the Plaster Wall?

This behavior probably indicates a nutritional deficiency. Birds need not only calcium but also other minerals and trace elements that are present in the mineral blocks that are sold at pet stores. Even if the mineral block is completely ignored at first, don't take it out of the cage. Sometimes a bird pays no attention to the mineral block for months and then suddenly starts gnawing on it and reduces it to nothing within a few days. Nibbling on eggshells is no substitute for a mineral block. Eggshells do contain calcium but none of the other minerals and trace elements the birds need. Still, they enjoy pecking on eggshells. If possible, give your bird only shells from chickens that were organically raised and were not fed fish meal.

Is It All Right to Let a Parakeet Nibble on Zwieback?

Eating a little zwieback does no harm to a parakeet as long as you don't give it too much. If you do, the bird will eat too little birdseed and fresh food—which are healthier—and get too fat. You can also give your bird a little stale bread. The crust is best, but always check to make sure there is no mold on it because mold is poisonous for birds.

What children ask: "How often does my parakeet need fresh water?" (Question from a ten-year-old boy.)
A bird has to have fresh, not too cold drinking water every day. The water has to be changed during the day if it gets dirty. The water dish should be cleaned every day.

Many pet parakeets are obese. Birds kept singly are especially given to eating out of boredom, but birds should not go hungry either. Give your bird fresh branches to gnaw on and fresh foods, let it fly free often, treat it with affection, and spend time playing with it.

If Your Bird Gets Sick

Pet parakeets are adversely affected if they are treated without love, if they are neglected, or if they live in a hectic or unsanitary environment. They are also subject to some minor ailments and serious illnesses but they have no way to let us know if they are feeling well, feeling pain, or are seriously ill. It is up to the person who looks after a bird to notice when its behavior changes either suddenly or gradually. If your parakeet shows no interest in its playthings for several days, if its usual happy chatter gives way more and more to silence, if a bird that ordinarily seeks the company of others suddenly keeps to itself, these are signs you should not ignore.

A Sick Parakeet

If a parakeet is sick it usually sits in its favorite spot with puffed-up plumage—body almost horizontal and tail slightly drooping—and shuns contact with other birds. With its bill buried in the back feathers, eyes dull and half closed, it rests on both feet, not balanced on one leg in the normal sleeping posture. A sick bird hardly eats but drinks more than usual. If the bird is not helped quickly it may get so weak that it is no longer able to hold onto its perch and falls to the floor. In such a situation there is no time to lose. A visit to your avian veterinarian is mandatory because such a small organism needs medical help quickly.

First Measures

Some diseases start on very gradually and can easily go unnoticed for some time. Luckily, as the daily experience of veterinarians shows, the dreaded serious diseases of birds occur relatively infrequently. Much more common are broken bones and dislocated wings, as well as injuries resulting from collisions, getting the foot band caught, overly long claws, or encounters with cats or dogs. Young parakeets are more susceptible to disease than older ones because their resistance is not yet fully developed. They are frequently subject to diarrhea, constipation, and colds. In anticipation of the day when you might need veterinary services, ask around soon after acquiring your birds where there is a vet experienced in treating birds. However, you have to act on your own when dealing with minor ailments and routine problems and in emergencies

Birds that are as active as these are healthy. A sick bird merely squats apathetically on its perch.

requiring first aid. The following recommendations should help you avoid making things worse.

Diarrhea

Sign: Watery droppings. Note: Diarrhea is *not* a disease but an outward symptom that something is wrong!

Cause: Many parakeets produce watery droppings after an overly cool bath, after a traumatic experience or an emotional loss, or after eating too much fresh food or food that was too cold.

Treatment: Give the bird some activated charcoal. Sprinkle it over the birdseed or—more effective—dissolve it in some water and introduce it into the beak with a syringe. Boiled, unseasoned rice also counteracts diarrhea. Give the bird weakly brewed, lukewarm black tea, weak camomile tea, or a few drops of Pepto-Bismol or Kaopectate. Omit all fresh food until the droppings are normal again. You may want to add a few drops of vitamin supplement to the drinking water and give the bird some fat-free crackers or stale white bread to exercise its beak on. Make sure the bird is kept evenly warm.

Warning: If the droppings are not only watery but also foamy, mixed with blood, or strangely discolored, consult a veterinarian immediately.

Constipation

Sign: The bird keeps straining and whips its tail sideways in an unsuccessful effort to pass droppings.

Cause: Obesity, abdominal tumor, intestinal blockage, grit impaction of the gizzard, dehydration (insufficient water to help soften the feces), or a retaining egg (pressure on the intestines).

Treatment: Take the bird in your hand and dab the vent with lukewarm water. If this does not help, mix a drop or two of cod-liver oil with the seeds to help lubricate the feces. A few chicory leaves also may help. Glauber's salt may be dissolved in the drinking water. Another good old remedy is to add ten drops of syrup of buckthorn to the water. Remove all sand and grit for 24 hours.

Warning: If constipation persists, take the bird to the vet. In a female, egg binding may be the cause (see Glossary), especially if she is laying her first egg. If this is the case, the cloacal area will be visibly bulging. Expose the bird to an infrared lamp (see How-to: First Aid, page 78). If heat fails to relax the tense muscles within two hours, the situation is critical, and the bird has to be rushed to the vet.

Regurgitating Seeds

Sign: Both male and female birds may regurgitate seeds.

Cause: Basically, birds regurgitate seeds to feed their young, but this behavior can also become part of the courtship display addressed to a surrogate partner. Males will try to feed their mirror image or some other object when they have no live partner, and females feed inanimate objects in place of the chicks they wish they had.

Warning: If a bird regurgitates not only kernels but also a foamy slime and does so not just occasionally but several times a day, it may be suffering from crop inflammation. This may be brought on by the ingestion of harmful or poisonous substances, by infections, thyroid congestion caused by the intake of too much sand and grit, lack of iodine, or food that is eaten too cold.

Treatment: Take the bird to the vet.

Frequent Sneezing

Sign: The bird sneezes a lot, sometimes with a secretion running from the nostrils.

Cause: Sneezing can be triggered by temperature fluctuations or excessively dry indoor air, or it can be the beginning of a cold.

Treatment: Make sure the bird is kept evenly warm and protect it from all drafts. If the nostrils are runny, clean with lukewarm water. See an avian veterinarian immediately. He or she will use an antibiotic or decongestant for the nose. Expose the bird to infrared light (see How-to: First Aid, page 78). If the bird sneezes only occasionally, it is simply clearing its nasal passages.

Warning: A serious cold accompanied by noisy breathing has to be treated promptly by a veterinarian.

Plenty of exercise in the form of clambering and especially of flying is the major ingredient in keeping birds healthy.

Labored Breathing

Sign: The bird breathes with difficulty and sometimes noisily.

Cause: Labored breathing may be caused by obesity resulting from lack of exercise.

Treatment: Make sure the bird gets plenty of fresh air, encourage it to fly as much as possible, and give it less spray millet to eat.

Warning: If the bird clutches a cage bar with its beak and hangs down from it, hoping to breathe easier through the stretched tra-chea, it is time to take it to the vet.

Parasites

Sign: The bird picks restlessly at its feathers and keeps scratching.

Cause: An infestation with parasites (see Glossary).

Treatment: The vet should prescribe a medication that acts specifically on the parasite in question. He or she should explain to you in detail how to use the medication and how, after treatment, to disinfect all the objects the bird has been in contact with.

Warning: If you also notice weight loss, feather plucking, and a dulling of the plumage, have the vet check for hormonal or metabolic disorders. If the tests are negative, the problem is probably psychological in nature and may be cured by introducing a second parakeet.

Leg and Wing Injuries

Sign: The bird limps, drags one leg, or has one drooping wing.

Cause: The bird may be bruised from a collision or a fight with a rival.

Treatment: Keep the bird isolated and evenly warm. If there is no improvement within 24 hours, take the bird to the vet.

Warning: If one wing hangs down uselessly or the bird refrains entirely from using one leg, you are probably dealing with a fracture or a dislocated joint and a vet must be consulted. However, similar symptoms are also caused by ovarian, testicular, or other tumors.

Swelling below the Skin

Sign: There is palpable bulge under the skin.

Cause: This thickening can be a slow, localized accumulation of fat, or it can be an incipient tumor.

Treatment: Take the bird to the vet to check the abnormality.

Bleeding Wounds

Sign: Blood issuing from a wound.

Cause: Contact with pointed objects or fights with rivals.

Treatment: Dab wounds immediately with ferrous chloride. The blood volume of a bird as small as a parakeet is 1/10 of a fluid ounce (3 ml) at most, and the loss of about a sixth of this can be fatal. Sprinkle the ferrous chloride on a clean tissue, place over the wound, and hold against it with gentle pressure for about 60 seconds. Place the bird in a separate cage in a quiet place.

Warning: If the bird bleeds from the vent or the beak, it may have internal injuries and should be rushed to the vet.

Overgrown Claws or Upper Mandible

Sign: The bird gets its claws caught on things like curtains and gets hurt. The overgrown beak interferes with eating.

Cause: Claws or mandible are too long.

Treatment: Have the vet do the necessary trimming; don't attempt it yourself. There is too much danger of cutting into a blood vessel.

Concussion

Sign: The bird looks stunned or is unconscious.

Cause: The bird has collided with a window, a wall, or some object while flying.

Treatment: Place the bird in a box padded with soft paper, laying it on its right side. Put a cover with air holes poked into it on the box so that the bird rests in the dark.

Warning: If the parakeet doesn't recover within two hours, take it to the vet.

Changes in the Banded Foot

Sign: The foot with the band is swollen.

Cause: The bird may have had the band caught in something and yanked on the foot trying to free itself. If the swelling becomes too large, the band can cut off the blood flow to the foot.

Treatment: Keep checking the foot. If the swelling doesn't go down, take the bird to the vet and have the band removed.

Warning: Only a veterinarian should remove the band. Ask for a statement explaining the reason for removal and keep both the band and the vet's statement as documentation.

If Medication Has to Be Given

If you have to give your parakeet medication, be sure to conscientiously follow the vet's instructions concerning dosage, length of treatment, and method of administration. Ask the vet to explain how best to get the bird to take the medication. Following are some recommendations for giving various forms of medication:

Liquid or powdered substances can be sprinkled over sprouted seeds or dissolved in the drinking water.

Tablets should be crushed into a powder. If

you add medication to the drinking water or to tea, make sure the bird doesn't satisfy its thirst by eating fruit and vegetables. If you have to make the parakeet swallow a medication, hold the bird loosely in your hand and dribble or sprinkle the medication onto the tongue. Grabbing the bird is easiest in a darkened room, where it can't see very well and won't get overly excited.

The following products and non-prescription drugs can be used as a first aid. Observe the instructions that come with them.

Pet stores sell special seed mixtures to aid the molting process. The mixtures, fortified with vitamins, enhance the birds' overall vigor and aid the growth of new feathers.

Your avian veterinarian sells the following:

• Eurax Cream—a solution you dab with a Q-tip on areas affected by scaly face. Be careful not to get it too close to eyes and nostrils. In serious cases the doctor will use Ivermectic (Equalan), an injectable medication.

• Niclosamide (Yomesan) (to treat tapeworm).

• Levamisole (Ripercol-L) (to treat intestinal roundworms).

• Vitamin supplements: Injacom (to treat vitamin A deficiency, to promote bone healing, and in the treatment of egg binding, soft-shelled eggs, and soft bones). Calphosan (injectable form of calcium), and D-Ca-Phos (vitamin D_3-calcium-phosphorus nutritional supplement).

• Flucytosine (Ancoban) (to treat aspergillosis).

• ^{131}Iodine (Iodotope Therapeutic) (to treat hyperthyroidism, and in the diagnosis of thyroid disorders).

• Lugol's solution (oral iodine solution used to treat various thyroid conditions.

• Eye drops for removing crusty deposits on the eyelids. They are also used for cleaning wounds and the vent. The drops must be guaranteed free of cortisone and antibiotics. Don't use camomile tea; its action is too strong.

• Ferrous chloride in the form of styptic powder.

Alarm Signals

If you notice any of the following signs, consult pages 78 and 79. Then take your bird to the vet at once.

• Staggering, trembling, and, possibly, falling off a perch.

• Cramping or signs of paralysis.

• Plumage on head and neck dirtied by phlegm tossed from the nostrils, or nostrils glued shut.

• Breathing accompanied by squeaking or whistling noises; hanging from a cage bar by the beak to facilitate breathing.

• Foamy droppings mixed with blood.

• Teary eyes or eyelids encrusted with a slimy secretion.

• Heavily bleeding wounds.

• Drooping limbs.

• Unnatural position of the head with the head either bent backward or tilted strongly to one side.

Close Observation Provides the Clues

Knowing the habits of your parakeet well—its likes, dislikes, and favorite treats—is the key to quick recognition of changes in behavior and to prompt initiation of treatment if called for. A change in habits does not necessarily signal a serious illness. Often, temperature fluctuations or a frightening experience will temporarily alter a bird's behavior.

How-to: First Aid

When you notice that a parakeet is not well, place it in a cage of its own and let it rest, isolated from its companions, at an even, warm temperature. The use of a heat lamp often brings relief.

ulate blood circulation and the metabolism, thus aiding the elimination of unhealthy substances and activating the immune system. Check the temperature in the cage frequently. It should not rise above 95°F (35°C). Move the lamp farther away if necessary.

The bird should be given plenty of weak black tea to drink.

You should also set a bowl with steaming water near the

day, and then resume the exposure until the patient is visibly improving.

Before turning off the lamp: Let the temperature in and around the cage drop very gradually to room temperature. This should take two to three hours. During this time the lamp is moved away from the cage a few inches at a time. When you turn off the heat lamp altogether, drape a cloth over half the cage so that there will be a dark, absolutely draft-free corner the bird can retreat to.

A Visit to the Avian Veterinarian
Photos 2 and 3
If your parakeet's condition does not improve within a few hours, you have to take it to the vet. The bird should be placed in a small cage for the trip. Strap a rubber hot-water bottle to the long side of the cage with a heavy rubber band (see Photo 2) to provide warmth and comfort in cold weather. During the summer this is necessary only on cool days.

Place the cage in a cardboard box with plenty of air holes, and take the shortest route to the vet's office. If you don't have a car and don't want to have to cope with complicated public transportation, you can in many cities call an "animal" taxi.

In case of leg or wing fractures: If a bird with a broken wing or leg has to be transported, remove the top of the cage and all the perches, toys, and food dishes in the upper part. Fill

1. **A sick parakeet needs the even warmth provided by an infrared heat lamp set up outside the cage.**

Using a Heat Lamp
Photo 1
An infrared lamp of 150 to 250 watts is set up about 16 inches (40 cm) from the cage and aimed in such a way that its rays reach only about half of the cage. This allows the bird to move into the cooler half if it gets too warm or if the exposure is not beneficial. Infrared rays penetrate beneath the patient's skin, provide warmth, and stim-

cage to provide sufficient humidity.

Important: If there are signs of paralysis—the bird drags one foot or a wing hangs down uselessly—or if there is cramping, exposure to a heat lamp is harmful. Call your avian veterinarian immediately.

How long should you use the lamp? If necessary, leave the lamp on for two days and nights without a break. Turn it off for a

2. If you have to take your bird anywhere, protect it well against the cold.

the bottom tray with plenty of soft, crumpled paper, and place the bird in the middle of it (see Photo 3). Put the top of the cage back on, and make the trip as described above.

Questions the Vet Will Ask
- How old is the bird?
- What pet store or breeder did it come from?
- When did it first look unwell to you?
- What, specifically, did you notice in the bird's behavior?
- Has the bird been sick

before? Was a specific illness diagnosed?
- Who treated it and what measures and drugs were used?
- What birdseed mixture does the bird get? (Take a sample with you.)
- What other foods does it get?
- What does it drink?
- Has it recently eaten fruit or vegetables?
- Could it have gnawed on something containing toxic substances?
- What other pets live in your household?

Five Basic Rules to Follow if Your Bird Gets Sick
1. Isolate the bird, provide quiet and warmth, and, if the bird is unconscious, keep it in the dark.
2. Expose it to a heat lamp.
3. Consult an avian veterinarian as soon as possible.
4. Follow your vet's recom-

3. A bird with broken bones should be placed on some soft, crumpled paper.

mendations conscientiously.
5. Give drugs exactly as prescribed by the vet, and make sure you obey instructions concerning dosage and length of treatment strictly.

A Reminder about Sanitation
After any illness, but especially after contagious diseases, you have to thoroughly clean not only the cage and the bird's perch outside the cage, but also all objects it has any contact with. After cleaning them, treat them with a disinfectant, following manufacturer's instructions. Wash the disinfected items well in warm water and let them dry. "Safe" disinfectants are: Betadine (against some viruses, fungi, and bacteria), Clorox (also very effective against viruses, fungi, bacteria, and protozoa), Lysol (effective against most bacteria, and enveloped viruses, such as poxvirus, but ineffective against nonenveloped viruses, and will not kill most bacteria), and Nolvasan (against fungi, some bacteria, and enveloped viruses).

4. The foot of this baby parakeet is crippled. A vet has to determine the cause and may, perhaps, be able to help.

Questions Related to Health

Most parakeet owners consider their bird part of the family and are very concerned about its health and happiness. Many diseases can be prevented if parakeets are kept properly. The better the overall condition of a bird, the more likely it is to recover if it should get sick in spite of good care. Spending time regularly with your bird is essential to its well-being.

Watching some interesting activity from above.

Is it Bad for a Parakeet to Spend All Its Time in a Cage?

Flying keeps a parakeet healthy and happy. Parakeets fly not only swiftly but also over long distances. In nature, they fly to their feeding grounds and watering places and rely on their wings to escape predators. They oil their plumage thoroughly and painstakingly to make it water repellent. This is the only way birds have to keep from getting soaked in the rain and thus being rendered unable to fly. A parakeet that is not allowed out of its cage languishes and gradually loses interest in its surroundings. It may overeat or start plucking its feathers out of boredom. That is why every parakeet should be given the opportunity to fly extensively every day. As it is, birds can practice their inborn flying skills only to a limited degree in our living quarters. Anyone unwilling or unable to spend considerable time keeping a parakeet company and to create conditions that reflect its natural needs at least partially by allowing for flying, playing, gnawing, bathing, and preening should not keep birds at all.

Why Does My Parakeet Pluck Its Tail Feathers and Sleep Upside Down?

Feather plucking may be a protest against not being allowed out of the cage enough. Watch to see if it still plucks its feathers if it is allowed to fly free. If the bird keeps busy outside the cage and stops plucking itself, the logical solution is to let it out of the cage more often. If a parakeet sleeps hanging upside down from the cage roof, it is certainly not exhibiting normal behavior, but I do know several birds with this habit. It may also, however, be a way of asking for more attention.

Can I Catch a Cold from My Parakeet or Vice Versa?

You don't have to worry about catching your bird's cold, nor is yours contagious to the bird. The only bird disease infectious to humans is psittacosis (see Glossary and the Warning on the last page). The symptoms of psittacosis resemble those of the flu or a light case of pneumonia. Even a cold can be dangerous to a bird. Set up a heat lamp immediately (How-to: First Aid, page 78). Make sure when you air the room that no draft reaches the bird and that there is no major change in temperature. It is best to move the parakeet to a different room before you air. If it's freezing outside, keep the cage not too close to a window. Even a bath in water that is too cool can give a bird a cold.

My Parakeet's Droppings are Sometimes Watery. What Should I Do?

Try sprinkling a little activated charcoal over the birdseed every day, and withhold all fresh food until the droppings are normal again. If there is no improvement, take the bird to the vet. Watch closely to see when the droppings are watery. Many parakeets produce watery droppings after exposure to temperature fluctuations, after a cool bath, out of loneliness, and in reaction to separation from a partner or to changes in the environment.

What children ask: "My parakeet often sits on its perch in the cage, nodding its head vigorously. Why does it do that?" (Question from a nine-year-old girl.) Your parakeet is eager for company—the company of another parakeet or of a trusted human. A mirror or a plastic bird can help it pass the time during periods when "its" human is busy with other things.

The radiation from a television set is not exactly harmful to parakeets. Still, a bird's sleeping place should not be directly in front of the glimmering screen. The constant flickering and noise can make a bird extremely nervous.

Parakeet Offspring

Many parakeet owners, when they see their birds billing and cooing and preening each other lovingly and observe the cock busily feeding his mate, develop a desire to let their birds have offspring.

Breeding in the Regular Cage

When you notice your birds engaging in courtship behavior, the first thing you need to do is get a nesting box (see How-to: Incubation and Rearing Aids, page 92). The best place for the box is on the outside of the cage; inside it takes up too much room. Also, you'd be able to look into it only with difficulty, and you'd interfere too much with the parents when you perform the necessary cleaning tasks so close to them. You can also hang the nesting box on a wall immediately next to the cage, preferably at a height that allows for easy inspection of the nest. Whatever location you decide on, the cage door should remain open during the incubating and brooding period, so that the birds are free to fly a lot and can get back and forth unhindered between food dishes and nesting box.

From "Whispers of Love" to Mating

When you give a parakeet pair that is already in a breeding mood a nesting box, you set a preprogrammed process in motion. The female will first approach the box warily and then examine it more and more throroughly. The male, too, will take a brief look, but he leaves it up to the female to make the necessary adjustments. She will chip away a little on the inside walls and perhaps at the entry hole and gradually spend more and more time inside the box.

The scenario is different if you combine two birds that don't yet know each other, hoping that they will produce offspring. The female is often unresponsive at first or reacts with irritation to the courting cock. The latter then has to proceed with infinite patience, circling the hen with tiny steps, tapping her shoulder timidly with his bill, bowing before her, and touching bills, head and neck feathers standing up on end and pupils narrowed with passion. If the birds are on the floor, he will then try to step on her tail, to which she objects with loud screeching. He will also

These two cocks are quite impressive fellows, but shy. Let's see which one manages to win the hen.

Soon the pair will start to bill and coo and to scratch each other's head in leisurely fashion. Then it won't be long before love-making.

drum against wood in front of her and try to impress her with a trilling song. He comes up to her repeatedly to nibble at her head feathers and tries to feed her with his bill, held at right angles with hers.

Mating Mood

Once the hen has overcome her distrust of the cock, she will let him rest and sleep next to her, accept food from his bill, allow him to preen her head feathers, and follow him from perch to perch. Occasionally a hen takes the initiative. She approaches the startled male, begging food the way nestling birds do, seeks to be close to him, and keeps holding out her head and neck for him to preen. If both birds are still quite young, it often takes months before the lifelong bond is formed and the birds come into breeding condition.

When the courtship displays have finally aroused the hen's sexual interest, she assumes the copulating position, balancing horizontally on a perch with her head thrown way back and her tail raised. In a state of great excitement the cock then mounts her lower back, wraps one or both wings around her body, and holds onto her neck feathers with his bill. In a precarious balancing act the birds then press their cloacas against each other so that the cock's semen can enter the hen's oviduct.

The First Egg Is Laid

The birds copulate several times before the hen lays her first egg. Probably you won't even be aware when that happens because, at this point, she is spending most of her time in the nest box and emerges only to eat and deposit droppings. Before the first egg is produced you might almost get the impression that the female is sick. She often looks very slim, as though frightened, and she may occasionally raise her wings and tremble. The droppings are very soft and produced in large quantities.

Laying eggs is incredibly draining for the female. Anyone who has witnessed the process knows how hard it is for the bird afterwards to retain her balance on the perch. She looks extremely thin, holds her wings slightly away from the body, sways, trembles, and bites into the air, presumably to calm her breathing. But after a few minutes she recovers.

Making love takes practice, too! Keeping one's balance is not all that easy.

A five-day-old chick, quite naked.

This chick is about 12 days old.

The age difference between the 10- and 16-day-old chicks is clear.

Shortly before an egg emerges you can see a slight bulge in the lower abdomen near the vent. If the female then suddenly emerges from her box and sits on the cage floor, whips her tail and strains without producing the egg, you have to assume that she is suffering from egg binding. Immediately supply even warmth by turning on a heat lamp, and raise the air humidity (see How-to: First Aid, page 78). If the hen doesn't produce the egg within an hour or two, rush her to the vet.

In most cases, though, the eggs are laid without complications. Restrain your curiosity and don't try to peek into the nest box. During the first few days, the female is very sensitive to disturbances of any kind, including too much activity in the room and loud noises. She might react by leaving the box and laying no more eggs. If she is not interrupted, she will go on laying every other day until she has a clutch of four to six eggs. A well-fed hen in good condition may lay as many as nine or ten.

The eggs of parakeets, like those of all cavity brooders, are pure white. They generally weigh about 2.7 grams in the case of cage birds; eggs of wild parakeets in Australia weigh about 2 grams.

If you get a chance to peek into the nest box while the female is absent from it, resist the temptation to touch the eggs even if they are dirty. This is important because the eggs are covered with a wax-like film that protects the embryos against infections and must not be tampered with.

Busy Incubating

Many parakeet females settle down to brood as soon as the first egg is laid. They then sit on the eggs steadily day and night, leaving only to void. A brooding hen produces excreta only about four or five times a day, not every 12 to 15 minutes as normal. Now, however, the droppings are bigger and heavier. When returning to the box after a few minutes' absence the female checks the eggs by feeling them with her brood patch (see Glossary), a small area on the abdomen that has almost no feathers. At regular intervals she moves the eggs that are in the center of the nest hollow outward toward the edge and rolls the outer ones to the center. Thus, the eggs are turned, and each in turn benefits from the greatest warmth at the center of the nest. All the eggs have to be incubated an average of 18 days. If the female starts brooding after the second egg is laid, the egg laid first will hatch after 20 days; if she starts immediately after the first egg appears, this first egg will hatch after 18 days. Then, following the pattern of egg laying, another chick will hatch every other day.

During this entire period the cock feeds the hen through the entry hole, inviting her there with special calls. When not feeding his partner, he always stays close to the nesting box, keeping guard. Some hens allow the male into the box during incubation, where he then settles down close to his mate.

Are the Eggs Fertile?

Not every egg in the clutch is necessarily fertile. Young pairs are not always successful at fertilization. Malnourished parakeets, too, sometimes lay "clear" eggs, as breeders call unfertilized eggs. You can check the eggs after the sixth day by holding them up against a bright flashlight. You can tell a fertile egg by the dark nucleus and the fine red veins running through the egg. By contrast, sterile eggs are entirely translucent. Leave the sterile eggs in the nest because their removal might upset the hen. Only if there are six or more eggs in the nest should you try to remove a sterile egg and a few days later perhaps another one.

New Life Stirring

After incubating about 18 days, the embryo has developed into a viable chick. By then, the food supply inside the egg has been used up. On its upper mandible, the chick has a thorn-like protuberance, the so-called egg tooth. With its help, it is able to break out of its shell. About 24 hours before emerging, the chick announces its impending appearance with soft chirps and scratching noises. Rotating millimeter by millimeter, the chick perforates, or pips, the shell with its egg tooth. This turning catches the mother's attention. She repeatedly looks over all her eggs, checks the shells with her tongue, and finally concentrates on the egg in which life is stirring. Most chicks succeed through tireless pushing and stretching motions in breaking the shell along the pipped line. They free themselves of the halfshell in which they are still stuck by kicking with their legs and wings, and they immediately seek the protective warmth of the mother's plumage.

Not all chicks are strong enough to emerge from the shell without help. The egg membrane may have dried out and stuck to the chick, or it may take too long before oxygen reaches the chick through the cracks and holes in the shell. If the parakeet mother fails to help at this point, the chick is lost. But

At about 18 days, the colors already begin to show.

parakeet hens are programmed by nature to assist the hatching process. They crave the taste of egg membrane. The hen will reach with her beak into the hole the chick has pecked and break out a piece of the shell. This provides the chick with air and helps it break out of the shell altogether, and at the same time satisfies the mother's appetite for egg membrane. The female moves the pieces of shell to a corner away from the nest cavity or out of the box altogether, for the naked nestlings might hurt themselves on the sharp edges. Occasionally, a female neglects to remove a shell. When you check the nesting box you should take out any shells that are still there.

Feeding the Chicks

Soon after the chick has recovered from the immense effort of hatching and has warmed up sitting under the mother's plumage, it will announce that it is hungry by kicking and squeaking. The mother responds by pushing her bill against the chick's until the baby bird is lying on its back, its bill pointing straight up. The youngest chicks get the so-called "crop milk," a nutritious secretion from a gland in the mother's crop. From the third day on, some predigested food from the crop is mixed with the milk. For the actual feeding, the mother places her beak at right angles over the chick's. With a rapid vibrating motion of the head and a push of the tongue, the seeds, enveloped in saliva, are sent sliding into the chick's small beak.

Baby Parakeets in Australia

Although wild parakeets are used to extremes of climate in central Australia, the brooding hens suffer when the temperature is 104°F (40°C) or more in the shade. They get up from the nest, where the chicks doze lethargically, to gasp for air and pant at the entry hole. The rapid breathing makes moisture evaporate from the mucous membranes of the pharyngeal cavity. This is the way birds, which do not sweat like humans, cool down.

For the first few days the chicks are fed lying on their backs, and the feedings are as frequent during the night as during the day. That's why you should always leave a small light on so that the female can see what she is doing. If there are several chicks in the nest, they all lie on top of each other in a heap, with the youngest at the bottom and the oldest at the top. Very young chicks are fed only when they beg; older ones get food regularly without having to ask for it. As the chicks get older, the feeding behavior of the mother begins to change. When they are about eight days old, the young are hardly fed anymore at night, and from about the fourth to the sixth day on they are no longer always fed in a supine position but begin to squat on their tail ends. From about 10 to 12 days on, they sit up for the entire feeding. At this point, too, the father helps with the feeding of the older chicks—if the female lets him into the nest box. The mother now resumes eating from the food dishes.

The Warmth and Safety of the Nest

Since the male continues to bring food to the female during the nestling period, the mother bird has to leave the nest only rarely. She can thus keep the chicks warm under her wings and defend them if necessary. The mother's body warmth is especially important during the first few days because it is hard for the newborn chicks to maintain a constant body temperature. Small and naked, they need the mother's warmth. Thus, the hen spends practically all her time sitting on her chicks during the first few days, covering them completely with her spread wings and keeping them warm until they develop feathers of their own. She continues to brood until the youngest chick is 16 days old and only then begins to leave the nest box more frequently.

If several pairs raise young together in an aviary, each parakeet mother always fiercely defends her chicks. A strange female that pokes her head in the entry hole is immediately hacked at by the hen sitting on the nest. Real fights can break out, in which the birds can get hurt. Defense of the brood is necessary to ensure the survival of the young. If a strange female succeeds in penetrating into the nest, she may kill the entire brood.

Is Everything as It Should Be in the Nest?

The nest should be checked at least once a day, preferably when the mother has left it for a moment, as a chick might have died. The body would decay quickly and endanger the health of the other chicks. You should also make sure that all the chicks are developing properly, that is, that they are growing properly, gaining weight, and beginning to develop feathers. Feel the crops of the baby birds carefully. If they feel empty, the young birds may not be getting enough food. If that is the case, you may have to institute supplementary feedings or hand-rear the chicks (see How-to: Incubation and Rearing Aids, page 93).

The Chicks Are Thriving

Parakeets are typical altricial birds, that is, their young hatch at an immature and helpless stage. They are blind and completely naked at birth and thus depend on the mother's care for survival. This is in contrast to precocial birds, such as chickens, which follow their mother and forage for food immediately after hatching.

1st to 5th day: The newly hatched chick weighs from 2 to 2.7 grams. Its eyes are still closed. It is fed lying on its back.

6th to 8th day: The chick now weighs 12 to 14 grams. The egg tooth is shed.

7th day: The wing feathers begin to grow in.

8th day: The chick can hold its head up and take a few steps. It is only rarely fed at night now.

9th day: The tail feathers are growing in. The eyes open. The chick usually sits on its tail now for feedings. When it has had enough, it no longer squeals but hides under the mother's wing.

12th day: The chick is now covered with down and weighs about 23 grams.

17th day: The chick already weighs slightly over an ounce (34 g). All the feathers are coming in but are still stuck inside their sheaths.

21st day: The first feathers unfold and display their colors. The chick runs around in the box and begs for food.

28th day: The wing feathers have grown almost to their full length, and only the tail feathers are still quite a bit shorter than those of the parents.

28th to 31st day: The nestlings have become accomplished climbers, flap their wings, and push out of the entry hole. They now weigh about 1⅓ ounces (37 g).

32nd to 35th day: The fledglings are practicing flying and landing and try to eat on their own, although the father still feeds them.

38th day: The plumage is fully developed, but the colors are less bright than those of adult birds.

3rd to 4th month: First molt. The birds emerge from this post-juvenal molt with fully developed, adult plumage and are now sexually mature.

6th to 8th month: The young birds are mature enough to mate and form a lasting pair bond.

Close examination is essential.

The hen takes a look at the nesting box.

Banding

Although in the United States parakeets are not required by law to wear a foot band, bands are useful for identification purposes, and pedigreed birds are routinely banded. Get the bands ahead of time so that you can put them on the birds when they are five to ten days old (see How-to: Incubating and Rearing Aids, page 93).

I recommend the use of closed metal rings because the year of birth can be stamped on them. This is of interest to some buyers of young parakeets.

Important: After banding the first chick you should watch for the reaction of the parents before banding the rest of the chicks. Sometimes the parents resent this foreign object and try to bite it off, which can result in the loss of a foot. If you notice such aggressive behavior, remove the band immediately,

and band all the chicks after they have reached independence.

Sanitation in the Nest Box

Most parakeet females remove droppings and other debris from the nest box or collect them in a corner where they can easily be disposed of. However, some make no effort to clean the nest, and you have to do it for them.

Carefully remove the nestlings and place them in a box lined with warmed paper. Start by cleaning the nest hollow in the box. Then pour a little over 1 inch (3 cm) of hamster or cat litter into the box to serve as nesting material (see How-to: Incubation and Rearing Aids, page 92). If necessary, clean the feet and toes of the chicks every day with a damp, soft paper towel because caked dirt can give rise to malformations.

The nesting box should be disinfected and thoroughly washed with hot water after every brood.

Hygiene is no problem for parakeets living wild in Australia. The female flies some distance away to deposit her droppings so as not to attract a predator's attention to the nest, and the baby birds' excreta dry quickly in Australia's hot climate. Scientists also think that the nests of parakeets—like those of other parrots—contain small moths that feed on the young birds' excreta. This surprising symbiosis has been shown to exist in the nesting chambers of the golden-shouldered parakeet *(Psephotus chrysopterygius)*, which nests in termite mounds. The small termite larvae not only consume the excreta in the birds' nest but also keep the baby birds' feet and feathers clean. Since parrots in general make no attempt to keep the nest sanitary, it is quite likely that similar forms of symbiosis exist in all species.

The Young Leave the Nest

After the nestlings have reached the age of about four weeks, you will notice that they appear more and more often at the entry hole and examine their surroundings. You can also hear them beating their wings. They are exercising their flight muscles—a sign that they are getting ready to leave the nest. Even though the young birds are already strong and quite agile, they still have to practice to achieve full mastery of the air. A young bird leaving the nest for the first time can propel itself through the air by flapping its wings, but aiming for a landing place and reaching it safely still represents a major challenge.

My advice: Put up some hemp ropes in the room, and stick some branches solidly in flower pots to provide the fledgling birds with some easy landing sites. You can also cover walls or pieces of furniture with reed mats the birds can grab onto. Although the young are able to fly and fend for themselves when they leave the nest, the father still feeds them for two or three weeks, until they are able to eat without any help at all. You can assist this process by spreading crushed seeds on the floor and offering them in cups in such a manner that the young birds can get at them easily. By eating these partially prepared seeds, the youngsters gradually learn to remove the husks themselves. You should also offer them sprouted seeds and fresh food. And it goes without saying that the birds should get fresh water daily.

Don't forget: When you sell or give away a bird, write the name and address of the new owner, as well as the bird's band number in your record book.

Everything seems to be satisfactory.

If you would like your parakeets to reproduce, you will have to give them a nesting box because females try to breed only rarely without such a box. In the rare case where this does happen, the hen will first find a hiding place, such as a box, a space on top of furniture, or behind books, or she may simply drop her eggs on the cage floor. Then she pays no further attention to them or even breaks them.

Material: The floor of the box should preferably consist of hardwood, the sides, of ³/₈ to ³/₄ inch (1–2 cm) thick boards or plywood half that thickness. Spruce or pine is best because it regulates the moisture. Particleboard should not be used because it contains chemicals that can be toxic to the birds.

Finishing: The entry hole (see Photo 1) should measure 2 inches (5 cm) across and be located to the side of the nest hollow, so that the female doesn't land on

(2 cm) deep. The roof of the box should flip open to facilitate nest checks and cleaning.

Location: The box is best mounted on the outside of the cage because it takes up too much room inside. Cut a hole the size of the entry hole in the grating of the cage, and attach the box securely to the cage. You can close the hole in the cage later with galvanized wire. You can also hang the nesting box on a wall next to the cage.

Raising birds in an aviary: Don't hang the nesting boxes too closely together in the aviary to avoid conflict between the females. A distance of 6 feet (1.5 m) is ideal. Mount all the boxes at the same height; the highest ones are always the most popular ones.

1. The entry hole is the right size.

2. The perch below it is used for feeding the hen.

A Nesting Box for Parakeets
Photos 1 and 2
Each breeding pair needs its own nesting box. In colony breeding, each breeding pair should have a choice of boxes to prevent fighting. You can build nesting boxes yourself or buy them at pet stores.

Format: A box 10 inches (25 cm) long, 6 inches (15 cm) deep, and 6 inches (15 cm) tall is ideal.

the eggs when she enters the box. The entry hole is used by the male during the entire incubation period for feeding the female, and a perch should therefore be added to the outside of the box a little below the hole (see Photo 2). Inside the box there should be a block with a concave nest area hollowed out about 3–4 inches (8–10 cm) in diameter and about ³/₄ inch

Nesting Materials
Photo 4
In their native Australia, parakeets breed in tree holes. They don't build nests but make do with the rude accommodations nature provides. You therefore don't need to offer your birds nesting materials. Wait until the young hatch, and then cover the bottom of the box with about 1¹/₄ inches (3 cm) of cat litter or pine chips to keep things sanitary. Never use sawdust or cedar chips.

Banding the Chicks
The chicks should be banded when they are about 7 days old. Here is how to do it:
• Hold the chick loosely in your hand. Stretch up one foot

with your thumb and index finger and slip the band over the three longest toes.

• Move the band up the leg until, pressed close to the leg, it passes the last toe.

• Let go of the band. All the toes are now below it.

Supplemental Feeding/Hand Rearing

Photo 3

During your daily nest check, feel each chick's crop with gentle pressure. If you repeatedly find chicks with empty crops and these chicks fail to grow properly, they are getting too little food from their parents.

Supplemental feeding: Give the chicks extra feedings until they are 14 days old, using a feeding syringe you can buy at a pet store. After that, feed the chicks rearing food (see page 99) with a small spoon. To do this, remove the chicks from the box one at a time, set each down on some soft paper, feed it, clean it

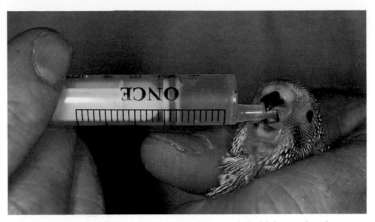

3. A syringe is helpful if you have to hand-rear small chicks or give them supplemental feedings. You can feel when the crop is full.

off with a paper towel dampened with warm water, and put it back in the nest.

Hand rearing becomes necessary if the parents refuse to feed the chicks altogether. Here the chicks have to be separated from the parent birds. Make sure they are kept at an even temperature and constant humidity.

Food: The following dry mixture should be reduced to a fine powder (use a blender!), then mixed with warm (100–108°F) water to a thin cream. The ingredients can be obtained in a health food store or pet shop.

• 3½ tablespoons of high

protein baby cereal,

• 1½ tablespoons wheat germ,

• 1½ tablespoons of millet meal,

• 1½ tablespoons of sunflower meal,

• 5 drops of a multivitamin (sold at pet stores).

Pet stores also sell ready-made rearing and hand-feeding diets.

Feeding times: Until the eighth day, every two hours, including at night. From the ninth day on every three hours, now only from 6:00 A.M. until midnight; from the fourteenth day on, every four hours. Mix the food fresh twice a day and keep it in the refrigerator between feedings. Warm each portion to 97° F (36° C) in a baby-bottle warmer before giving it to the birds.

The right amount: While feeding every two hours, give each chick about one tablespoon at a time; during the three-hour interval phase, two tablespoons; and during the four-hour interval phase, as much as the chick will eat. Weigh the birds daily and record their weight gain. If a chick fails to gain weight steadily, it is getting too little food.

4. This posture is typical of young birds that are almost ready to fly. When they are afraid, they squeeze into a corner of the nesting box.

Breeding Parakeets

I t is not uncommon for parakeet pairs to reproduce without the owners having had any intention of raising baby birds. Such unplanned events have turned many bird lovers into enthusiastic breeders. Although parakeets don't necessarily require special conditions to reproduce, the breeder should nevertheless have a basic knowledge of parakeet breeding if he or she cares about the well-being of the birds. One aspect that definitely requires some advance planning is what to do with the young birds. Anyone who has been breeding birds for several years will probably also become interested in exhibiting birds.

Housing Breeding Pairs

Before a pair of birds can breed you have to prepare a space where they can do so without disruptions. There are four possibilities:

An indoor aviary measuring about 48 x 40 x 72 inches (120 x 100 x 180 cm) is large enough for two pairs. Indoor aviaries as well as prefabricated parts you can assemble yourself are available from pet dealers.

A bird room can accommodate four to six pairs, depending on its size. You have to make very sure, though, that the room is absolutely "bird-proof" (see page 41). The room should have a tile or cement floor that is easy to clean.

An outdoor aviary attached to a shelter that can be heated is appropriate for raising a small flock and can serve as year-round accommodations. This arrangement is most in tune with the parakeets' natural pattern of breeding in colonies.

For a bird room or an aviary you should figure on about 10 square feet (1 m²) per bird. This way there will be no overcrowding, which can cause stress and fighting among the birds.

Important: If you want to build an outdoor aviary and shelter, you will need a building permit, and you should consult your neighbors. Building such a structure is not cheap and should be planned ahead in detail. Get in touch with breeders and breeders' associations for advice and to profit from their experience, and consult specialized literature (see page 138).

Special breeding cages in various sizes are

A hen that lets herself be fed with such enjoyment is unlikely to resist sexual overtures for long.

The cock feeding the hen is not just part of courtship display leading up to mating but also strengthens the permanent pair bond. If the cock is sick, the roles are sometimes reversed and the hen feeds her partner.

The blue cock is head over heels in love.

The yellow hen is still pretending indifference.

Discuss with your pet dealer what cages or other housing materials are available. Always keep in mind when you plan the space that the breeding pairs should not suffer damage from being overly confined during their exhausting breeding activities.

Mounting Nesting Boxes

Special breeding boxes and cages have the nest boxes already built in, but for an indoor aviary, a bird room, or the shelter of an outdoor aviary you will have to provide them yourself. You need at least two boxes per pair because the hens are very particular about choosing a nesting box. Serious conflicts can arise if two birds decide on the same box. If there are plenty of other boxes, the hen that loses out still has several to choose from, which helps restore her good mood. You can buy nesting boxes ready-made at pet stores or you can build them yourself. Boxes 10 inches (25 cm) long, 6 inches (15 cm) deep, and 6 inches (15 cm) tall have proven most successful. Both parents and a maximum of five chicks can fit into this size box (see How-to: Incubation and Rearing Aids, page 92). If the birds breed in a colony in an outdoor aviary, the boxes are mounted in the shelter because the nestlings are most protected there from the weather. Once the females have started incubating and have settled down on their eggs, the unused boxes can be removed.

Important: Always make sure that no unattached parakeets remain in the bird room or aviary. Cocks tend to irritate brooding hens by regaling them with unwanted courtship displays and are then attacked as rivals by the hens' mates. Single females sometimes try to destroy the eggs of a sitting hen and occasionally even kill baby chicks.

preferred by many breeders because they can be stacked and take up relatively little room. I myself am opposed to the use of breeding boxes and cages, where the birds are confined for weeks on end without an opportunity to fly while they incubate and rear the chicks.

Important: If you use breeding cages, you have to have a flying area of adequate size that the young and the parent birds can use once the chicks fledge.

Factors that Improve the Chance for Success

• Fresh, lightly circulating air in the breeding room but without the slightest draft.

• A constant room temperature between 59 and 64°F (15–18°C).

• An air humidity of 60%. Set up a humidifier, and don't hang the nesting boxes near radiators. During hot, dry spells, spray some water into the boxes every day with a plant mister.

• Long hours of daylight with some direct sunlight. This is best provided through open windows with screens.

• During cold spells, attach some light heating cables to the floors of the boxes on the outside.

• If the breeding pairs have acoustic contact among each other and perhaps see each other, this often increases their eagerness to breed.

Parakeets Suitable for Breeding

Parakeets that are going to breed should be young and healthy. You can tell suitable candidates by, among other things, their lively nature and the color of their ceres—bright blue or pink in the male, and beige in the female. The birds should not display temperamental weaknesses, such as nervousness, excessive timidity, or extreme aggressiveness. They have to be able to fly and climb well, use their voices to produce normal parakeet sounds, and keep their plumage in perfect shape. Although parakeets are sexually mature after only a few months, birds selected for breeding should be 10 to 12 months old before they are permitted to raise young. By then they are grown to full size and strong enough to endure the physical strain of reproduction. Pairs should be made up of birds from different breeders, that is, they should be genetically different, to preclude inbreeding.

Selecting Partners

As a rule parakeet pairs get along very well after an initial period of getting used to each other. If you already have a flock of birds in an aviary and observe them, you will notice quickly which cocks are interested in which hens. What counts here is not "love at first

Who wants to guess what colors the offspring will be?

sight," but the selection of a partner that promises successful mating and rearing of the young. In a compatible pair the partners are generally faithful to each other but exceptions are not infrequent, especially among domesticated parakeets.

If you would like to achieve specific breeding goals, you should combine only birds that have all the qualities required for attaining those goals (see pages 101 and 103). If no steady pairs form within the desired time period, pair the birds yourself and put each pair in a cage of its own. Watch the behavior of the birds carefully. A pair that fights constantly is not likely to start breeding. Sometimes irritation gives way to affection after a few days. If tension continues, a new male may please the female better. The rejected cock usually accepts his lot without fighting and happily settles for a different hen if one is provided.

Cinnamon light green (cock).

Three especially beautiful color varieties (see below, left).

Diluted yellow (cock).

In the photo above, right:
Rainbow (at top); Cinnamon
clearwing dark blue (on left);
Recessive pied olive green
(on right).

Clearwing GG dark blue (hen).

Two hens, on the other hand, would fight practically to the death over a single male. Pairs that have taken to each other in their cages may be returned to the aviary or bird room.

Watching the birds regularly is the best insurance against disruptions in the brooding and rearing process. As soon as anything unusual is noticed, the cause should be determined and eliminated.

What to Do if Difficulties Arise

Sometimes an egg develops a crack or a small hole. As long as the membrane beneath the shell is still intact, the egg can be saved. Take a small piece of shell from a broken egg and glue it onto the damaged spot with some egg white from a chicken egg or nontoxic white glue. It is important to prevent dehydration caused by increased entry of air.

Chicks that have difficulties hatching are usually assisted by the mother (see pages 87 and 88). Once they are hatched, the chicks occasionally don't get enough food or aren't fed at all. If that happens, you have to act. The best solution is to give a chick up to 12 days old to another brooding hen whose offspring are of about the same age. Older "orphaned" chicks can be completely hand-reared or given supplemental feedings (see How-to: Incubation and Rearing Aids, page 93).

It a female with young nestlings dies, the father might take over the parental care. If not, you should try, in this case too, to find another hen with chicks who might adopt the orphans. Luckily, parakeet females usually accept strange chicks and look after them as though they were their own. If this is not an option, you will have to hand-rear the chicks yourself.

Experience has shown that it is better not to leave more than five eggs in a nest. The baby birds develop better, and the strain on the parents is less. Mark the extra eggs with a crayon and place them in a nest with fewer eggs.

Tips on Feeding

Breeding birds, whether kept in an aviary or a

Diluted white-violet (hen).

cage, use up a great deal of energy raising young, and their diet therefore needs to be especially well planned and varied.

• Start introducing high-protein rearing food into the parent birds' diet two months before you expect them to breed. Add the rearing food twice a week. Pet stores sell various kinds of ready-made rearing food. Follow the manufacturer's directions for use.

You can also prepare your own formula as follows: Soften stale white bread (make sure there is no mold on it) in water; squeeze out the water and mix with an equal amount of chopped, hard-boiled egg yolk. Or mix fat-free cottage cheese with egg yolk and finely crushed zwieback in the proportion of 1:2:1. If the mixture is too thick, thin with a little carrot juice (available at health food stores). You can also add finely grated carrot to the mixture.

The proper amount: Give one teaspoonful per bird per day. Protein-rich food spoils quickly; therefore remove what is not eaten after about two hours. The daily menu also has to include fresh fruit and vegetables (see page 66), as well as sprouted seeds.

• Make sure there is always plenty of fresh drinking water available during the rearing period. Young chicks grow fast and require a lot of liquid—more than that supplied in the food.

• If there is no bird sand on the aviary floor, offer sand and grit in separate dishes and supply a mineral block.

Special Health Precautions

If a number of parakeets live together in the same space, there is a considerable danger of disease spreading among them. Birds in an aviary peck around on the floor and can easily pick up worm eggs and other pathogens. Droppings of wild songbirds and dirty food are a special source of danger. Worms undermine the health and debilitate birds, and they can also be disease carriers. That is why you should take the precaution of taking sample droppings from all the birds to the vet every six months to be checked. If necessary, perform wormings or other measures prescribed by the vet.

If you replace older breeding pairs with young birds from different breeders in order to introduce some new blood into the strain, the new birds should be kept in separate cages for ten days before they are combined with the birds you already have. This gives you a chance to assess the new parakeets' state of health and to have their droppings checked for pathogens and parasites.

Integrating New Birds into the Flock

If you keep your parakeets in pairs in individual cages, there is no problem of integration. But if you want to add new pairs to a flock in an aviary, first place the newcomers by pairs in cages that you hang at eye level in the aviary. This gives the young birds a chance to familiarize themselves with their new surroundings and the other birds. After about three days you can open the cage doors so that the pairs can get in and out of their cages at will. After a short while they usually feel at home in their new environment and are accepted by their fellows, so that you can remove the cages.

The Young Leave the Nest

The parakeet chicks leave the nesting box in the same order in which they hatched. Once they leave, they generally don't return again to the box. The father now keeps busy looking after the fledglings, feeding them usually for another two weeks, until they are able to eat regular food without any parental help. At this point all the young of the first brood should be housed in a separate aviary. The parents often begin right away to raise a second brood and would be disturbed in this by the older offspring. If one or two chicks of the first brood are still in the nest when the new eggs are laid, the hen often treats them badly, plucking their feathers. Here again it is important to keep a watchful eye. Remove mistreated chicks from the box and entrust them to the father's care. If the chicks are too young for this, try to give them to another breeding pair or rear them yourself.

How to Put an End to Breeding

When your parakeets have raised two broods, take down all the nesting boxes and move the birds to a common aviary, even if there are still eggs in some of the boxes. If you don't put an end to the breeding, parakeets may, under the favorable conditions of captivity, continue raising one brood after another and completely wear themselves out physically. Never permit more than two clutches per year, and always impose a rest period of six months between breeding cycles. During this rest period, the birds should be allowed to fly free as much as possible in the fresh air.

Nesting boxes, cages, aviares, and shelter now have to be cleaned thoroughly and disinfected (see How-to: Maintenance, page 58, and *Disinfecting* in the Glossary).

If you don't want to keep all of the young parakeets, you may be able to sell the unwanted ones to your pet dealer. The best time to pass them on is as soon as they are able to eat independently, or, about two weeks after they leave the nest. At this point they are, as breeders put it, "naturally tame."

Breeding Goals

The breeding of parakeets can be undertaken with any one of three different goals in mind. You may simply want to increase the number of birds; you may want to raise show birds; or you may want to produce birds of a certain color.

The novice breeder without specialized knowledge should start out with the simple aim of *raising healthy birds*. The young parakeets will be intended primarily as pets for bird lovers who like parakeets for their lively nature and colorful appearance but don't care about the exact size and the posture of their birds.

Someone breeding show birds will attempt to produce parakeets that conform to the standard defined by the UK Budgerigar Society by which show birds are judged (the American Budgerigar Society uses the standard set by the UKBS). If you are thinking

---

Not Just Green!

Breeders in Holland, Belgium, France, and Germany produced parakeets whose colors differed from the green of the wild birds. The first yellow parakeets were bred in Belgium in 1875; Germany followed suit in 1877. Efforts to breed pure blue parakeets first led to success in 1881, and lutinos were first reported in Europe in 1920. In Toulouse, France, the first dark green parakeet was bred in 1915, and in 1917 the first white one was reported.

---

about exhibiting birds you should definitely get in touch with the American Budgerigar Society (for address, see page 138) to find out what criteria show birds have to meet and to familiarize yourself with the complicated guidelines of evaluation. The following, partial list will give you some idea of what is called for:

• The ideal length is 8½ inches (21.6 cm) from the crown of the head to the tip of the tail.

• The overall shape or type of the bird has to taper gracefully from nape of neck to tip of tail, with an approximately straight back line and a rather deep, nicely curved chest.

• The head should be large, round, wide, and symmetrical when viewed from any angle. The curve of the head should start at the cere, from which point it rises upward and outward, continuing over the top and to the base of head in one graceful sweep.

• The beak has to be well "tucked into" the face, with the upper mandible protruding beyond the lower one.

• The wings should be carried just above the cushion of the tail without the tips crossing. They should measure 3¾ inches (9.5 cm) from the butt to the tip of the longest primary flight, which must contain seven visual primary flight feathers, fully grown.

• The tail should be straight and tight with two long tail feathers.

• The mask should be clear (that is, of uniform color), wide and deep, extend down below the chin, and have three round throat spots of even size evenly spaced on each side.

• The position (posture) should look secure and "natural," with the bird sitting steady on its perch, fearlessly upright at an angle 30 degrees from the vertical.

• The wavy markings on cheek, head, neck, back, and wings should stand out clearly and match the description of the bird's particular color strain.

In addition to conforming to these criteria, the bird has to be trained in good time before a show to sit in the prescribed small cages that have just two perches.

Among fanciers, these extremely large show birds are considered more "noble" than the wild parakeets of Australia! In order for all their bred "noble" traits to show up properly at an exhibition, birds are sometimes washed and combed or brushed with a shaving brush before they are displayed. This is necessary, however, only for the light-colored varieties.

Breeding for color aims at producing parakeets of pure color and with perfect markings. Any one breeder will probably concentrate on only a few varieties. Parakeets are at this point bred in about 80 colors plus many different markings.

The reader will have realized by now that breeding parakeets is no simple matter. It takes a great love for parakeets as well as a sense of responsibility, for, in my opinion, the exaggerated ambitions of breeders have created "monsters," such as the so-called featherdusters. These birds have feathers so long they look like wavy trains. Featherdusters seldom live beyond one year. But even birds that correspond to the regular show standard are considerably larger and heavier than normal parakeets (that is, parakeets that resemble their wild ancestors in size, body shape, and color). They, as well as birds whose colors differ widely from the natural coloration, are more susceptible to disease, and they tend toward obesity because most of them are awkward flyers. If one remembers what harsh environmental conditions parakeets have adapted to over the millennia in the Australian bush and how many natural catastrophes they have survived, one should, as a breeder, treat these enchanting little creatures with respect

and care. Let me quote just a little from the account of a journey in Australia by the dentist/ornithologist Dr. Hans Strunden:

"We had an opportunity to watch and admire hundreds of budgerigars. It seems to me that anyone who has once stood beneath one of these huge, thickly foliated budgerigar trees, has listened in amazement to the birds' voices resonating from the very top to the bottom, and has, after a while, been able to make out more and more of these small, green imps busily flitting around, peering out of holes, climbing out, or dashing back in—anyone who has experienced this will, I think, find it hard to admire man's attempts to apply his intellect and the knowledge of the Mendelian laws of genetics to these birds. Man has managed to turn these lively little creatures into veritable monsters and is not ashamed to display them confined in tiny boxes at exhibitions. And, to crown it all, show judges in all seriousness reward the results of these misguided efforts with prizes."

Keeping Breeding Records

Regardless of what your breeding goals are, keeping a breeding record is useful. You should note down which hen lays an egg and when, how big the clutch is, how many of the eggs are fertile, when the hen starts incubating them, when each of the chicks hatches, and, finally, when each of them is banded. Later you can complete the record by adding the sex and the color of the chicks. If you hand-rear chicks, also note down their daily weight gain. If you take a fertile egg from a clutch containing more than five eggs and put it in the nest of a pair with only three or four eggs, mark this egg with a nontoxic felt marker and then write down when, among its nest mates, this chick made its appearance. If you don't want to enter the data in the record book in the breeding room, jot the information down on a 3" x 5" card and transfer it to the record book later.

Introduction to Genetics

Success in breeding parakeets depends on many factors. A proper environment, a good diet, adequate care, and correct treatment of diseases are important, but so is an understanding of the laws of genetics. In order to achieve certain goals, the breeder has to know which color varieties can be paired. The laws of genetics are not easy to understand, I can try to convey only the basic principles here. If you want to learn more about this subject, consult the bibliography at the end of this book (see page 138).

Genes and Chromosomes

Parakeets, like all other creatures, pass on traits to their offspring in the form of genes. Genes are located in pairs on the chromosomes inside the cell nucleus. The genes determine such parakeet traits as the color and markings of plumage and body shape. Mitosis, the division of the cell nucleus, is the basis of cell reproduction, of the reproduction of the species, and of the passing on of genetic material. In addition to the chromosomes that function as carriers of general traits, there are somewhat differently built chromosomes that determine the sex of the offspring, the so-called sex chromosomes. In birds, the female has one X and one Y chromosome and the male has two X chromosomes. In humans, for example, it is the other way around: The female has two X chromosomes

These two birds are getting along beautifully. A mating is not far off.

and the male, one X and one Y chromosome. To the bird breeder, of greatest interest, apart from the sex of the birds, is, of course, their color.

Wild-colored Parakeets
Wild parakeets are mostly light green. The back, the wings, and the back of the head have the familiar brownish black shell markings. Only the mask—from the top of the head to the throat—is pure yellow, with six black dots on the throat and small blue to violet cheek marks. White patches on the five inner primaries form a white band when the wings are spread. The two long tail feathers are dark blue.

The green of the basic plumage can vary from yellowish to darker shades of green. Occasionally, yellow and blue parakeets have been sighted in the wild, but presumably these conspicuously colored birds quickly fall victim to predators.

How Do the Colors Originate?
What accounts for the colors of a parakeet's plumage? Feathers are composed of innumerable cells. The surface area of each feather is increased by vanes that extend on both sides of the central shaft and consist of many tiny rays, called barbs, which are branched and interlock with tiny hooks.

In each cell, an outer keratin layer surrounds the box-like cell wall, and the cell center is filled with a kind of marrow.

In a green parakeet feather, the outer keratin layer has the yellow pigment carotenoid incorporated in it, and the marrow contains the dark pigment melanin. The cell wall between the keratin layer and the cell center is colorless, but it is perforated by tiny tubes that reflect the light that strikes the feather. The red spectrum of the light is absorbed by the melanin, while the blue rays are reflected back. These rays pass through the carotenoid, which acts as a yellow filter, and makes the color appear green to our eyes.

The feathers of yellow parakeets have very little melanin stored in the cell marrow. Because of this, the blue is not reflected back and we see yellow instead of green. In the feathers of blue parakeets, by contrast, the keratin layer lacks the yellow pigment. This layer is white, and thus the blue is not changed into green. The feathers of white parakeets also have a white keratin layer; they lack carotenoid, and the marrow contains only small amounts of the dark melanin.

Two Genetic Factors Account for Four Colors
Thus, the four basic colors of parakeets go back to only two genes. The first is responsible for the production of yellow carotenoid (F) in the keratin layer, the second, for the storing of melanin (O) in the cell marrow. All green parakeets have both these genes; yellow birds have only the gene for carotenoid (F). Blue parrots, too, also have only one of these genes, namely the one for the melanin (O). White parakeets lack the F and the O gene.

The different color shades result in part from the interplay between the yellow pigment and the melanin, but the structure of the feathers also plays a major role.

Green Series and Blue Series
In the case of parakeets, breeders speak of a green series and a blue series because all color varieties go back to these two basic colors. Any mutation can appear in either color series and occurs in three degrees of intensity. The melanin (O) in the cell's marrow may be lacking (Ow), present in a single dose (Og), or present in double dose (On).

Green and blue parakeets with the dark wavy markings typical of the species have a double dose of melanin. When there is only one dose of melanin, the birds' colors appear lighter and the markings are gray, as in the green and blue graywings. If melanin is lacking or only minimally present, the birds are either yellow with a slight tinge of green or white with a slight tinge of blue and with barely visible markings, the so-called ghost markings.

There is also a brown factor (B), which is responsible for the darkening of the colors. All of the approximately 100 color varieties that are bred derive from these few factors. But how are the colors inherited?

Not every hen would put up with such boldness so soon. Maybe these two have been a pair all along?

Sometimes it takes a long time before the cock dares put his foot on the hen's wing. If the hen's resistance begins to weaken, the advances of the male become more urgent.

Dominant or Recessive?

Genes can be dominant or recessive. Green, for example, is always dominant over blue.

The following examples demonstrate this:

• If a green cock mates with a green hen, all the offspring are green. They have two identical genes for green = FF.

• If a green cock mates with a blue hen, green dominates. The offsprings are green, since green dominates. But the color blue is passed on in the form of a recessive gene. The offspring are "split," with two different color genes = Ff.

• If two green birds with split genes for color (Ff) mate, 50% of the offspring will have split genes (Ff), 25% will have two genes for green (FF), and 25% will have two genes for blue (ff).

Carotenoid can, like melanin, occur in varying intensity, that is, with two genes for it (FF), or with just one (Ff). If the yellow pigment is lacking altogether in birds of the blue series, the genes are ff. F is dominant over f. Thus, the color factor F is inherited in the following statistically predictable proportions:

• FF and FF (genes of the parent birds) = 100% FF (genes of the offspring).

• FF and Ff = 50% FF and 50% Ff.

• Ff and Ff = 25% FF, 50% Ff, and 25% ff.

• Ff and ff = 50% Ff and 50% ff.

• ff and ff = 100% ff.

Markings and the color intensity of markings are also inherited in dominant and recessive form. Thus, a double factor of melanin (On) is dominant over a single factor (Og) as well as over the reduced factor (Ow), with Og being dominant over Ow.

Technical literature on the laws of genetics uses the terms "homozygous" to indicate identical genes for a trait and "heterozygous" to indicate a gene pair made up of a dominant and a recessive part. Capital letters are used for dominant genes and lowercase ones for recessive genes. The parents are referred to as the P generation, and the first offspring are the F1 generation. If birds of the F1 generation are mated with each other (inbreeding), the young are called the F2 generation. If an F-generation bird is bred with a bird of the P generation, that is called backcrossing. This is done to reinforce a particular desired trait in the birds' appearance.

Sex-linked Genes

The gene for the dark pigment melanin is located on the X chromosome. The symbol for an X chromosome carrying a gene for melanin is X. If there is no gene for melanin on this chromosome, the symbol is "x°." X is dominant over x°. Males have two X chromosomes, females only one. In the case of females, it is therefore immaterial whether the gene for melanin is dominant or recessive; they always display the color carried on their X chromosome.

As you already know, a reduced dose of melanin results in light colors and ghost markings. A total absence of melanin produces lutinos in the green series and albinos in the blue series of parakeets. Lutinos are pale yellow and have a silvery white cheek spot. The cere is reddish violet in males as well as females, and the throat spots are lacking. The eyes of lutinos are red because there is no dark layer in the back of the eyes, and the blood therefore shines through, making the pupils look red, just as they do in white albinos.

Important: Only males can have split genes for the O factor. Females have only one X chromosome and consequently are always homozygous in respect to any sex-linked trait. Females thus always pass on the color indicated by the gene located on the X chromosome, whereas in males, the O factor can be present on both X chromosomes or just on one.

The young female is visibly startled by the unseemly aggressiveness of the mature cock.

Watching and Understanding Parakeets

If you make it a habit to watch your parakeet closely, you will learn a great deal about its behavior. You will soon recognize that your bird reacts to certain situations in certain ways, and, with a little intuition, you will begin to understand what its vocalizations and body language mean. The variety of behavior displayed by a pair is even richer because communication with other members of the species is naturally more complex. I have observed many parakeets over the past 15 years, and I think I can interpret their modes of expression fairly accurately. However, no parakeet is exactly the same as any other, and so you should not be surprised if you don't recognize the following descriptions of behavior in your bird in every detail.

What Does the Body Language Express?
Parakeets are incredibly agile and have amazingly perfect control of their bodies. They are fast and untiring flyers, climb easily both head up and upside down, and are able to reach all parts of the body except the head area with their bill when preening their plumage.

All kinds of frequently repeated actions parakeets engage in are part of what ethologists call comfort behavior. Comfort behavior includes activities related to body care, such as grooming and scratching, and movements, like yawning and stretching the wings, that serve to stimulate various body functions. Other forms of comfort behavior, like grinding the beak and stretching the legs backward, serve to break up periods of rest with some activity.

These repeated actions, in somewhat intensified or abbreviated form, are also used as body language.

Is this hen embracing the cock? It is more likely a case of a mismanaged landing.

If one bird lands awkwardly and too closely to another, both are very embarrassed afterwards and treat each other with special caution.

Body Language

Parakeets have an amazing physical agility. Their flexible joints allow them to go through contortions that look positively dangerous. This limberness comes into play during the daily preening, and it is also responsible for the acrobatic climbing the birds are capable of.

Preening the partner's head is like saying "I love you."

Parakeets raising their feet to scratch the head.

Reaching to the oil gland.

Raising the wings helps to cool down.

If two compatible parakeets live together, they communicate their moods and needs to each other. They often do the same thing at the same time, for instance, scratching, yawning, eating, and preening.

Both birds are busy preening themselves.

Grooming small contour feathers.

Rubbing the bill against a branch, too, is not done solely to keep it clean but also serves as a ritual of greeting. When a member of a flock returns to its partner after having been absent for some time, the latter greets it with beak rubbing.

After eating, the bill is rubbed clean on the perch.

Parakeets often start preening their small feathers in situations where two conflicting impulses cancel each other out, as when they are torn between fear and curiosity. Unable to decide on which urge to act, the bird engages in an apparently irrelevant "displacement" activity.

Yawning can be a sign of low oxygen.

Grooming the Plumage Is Not Everything

Grooming the plumage is not the only form of body care birds engage in. Other activities are also involved.

Scratching: When a parakeet scratches its head, it raises the leg under the wing, or from behind the wing, to reach the head and uses the claw of the longest toe for scratching. When it scratches the sides of the posterior body or around the vent, the foot is moved backward along the side of the body, and the two toes pointing forward are used for scratching. No claws are used because they could hurt the sensitive area around the vent. If a parakeet scratches a great deal, it may be because it has parasites. If the vent region is very dirty, the bird will also scratch a lot and draw your attention to the problem.

Head rubbing: Parakeets often rub their heads against the bars of the cage, perches, or other objects. This behavior is seen primarily in birds that are kept singly or in pairs that are not getting along very well. Presumably, head-rubbing parakeets are trying to make up for the lack of mutual preening. But the head may also be rubbed to relieve itching caused, for example, by mites.

Whetting the bill: Birds remove dirt and bits of food from the bill by whetting it against a perch or the cage bars. They do this after every time they eat, even if there is no food visible on the bill. If whetting does not clean the bill completely, the bird will resort to using the foot.

Shaking the feathers: Several times a day a parakeet will give its entire plumage a good shake. This is the way the bird gets rid of the dirt particles, bits of skin, and horny scales the bill has loosened in the course of grooming. A bird also shakes its feathers after a bath to shake off water and get the feathers to lie in their proper places, but shaking the plumage can also signal a mood change. If a bird is getting ready, after resting, to eat, fly, or gnaw on a branch, it often starts by shaking its feathers. Shaking also serves to release tension. If you come too close to your bird with an unfamiliar object, it will at first be afraid but then shakes itself when the object turns out to be harmless.

Between Rest and Activity

Grinding the bill: When a day ends in a completely relaxed mood, with the bird resting quietly on its favorite perch, you can often hear it grind its bill softly. This is a peaceful sound that indicates utter contentment.

Burying the bill in the back feathers: This is part of a parakeet's sleeping posture. If a bird assumes this position during the day, it wants to rest and be left in peace.

Resting on one leg: Parakeets normally rest on one leg when they sleep. The other foot is drawn up into the abdominal feathers, and the bill is buried in the back feathers. Parakeets sometimes also sleep while standing on both feet, but this can be a sign that the bird is sick. If a bird rests on one foot without sleeping, this means that it is not interested in any activities at that time.

Stretching the legs backward: After sleeping or a period of rest, a parakeet extends one leg and the wing of the same side backward. Then it does the same with the leg and wing of the other side. When the leg is pulled back, the toes often curl into a "fist" before the foot resumes its position on the perch. This sequence of motions is comparable to your stretching after having been in an uncomfortable postion for some time. Watch the feet of the bird when it stretches its legs. If it never curls its toes, this may indicate a weakness in the leg or foot muscles.

Lifting the wings sideways: Here the bird lifts and turns the closed wings sideways. This makes it look bigger, and birds often assume this posture to impress a female or intimidate a rival. If the bird makes itself extremely slender at the same time, however, this is a sign of extreme fear. And if, in addition, the legs are spread and tremble, the bird is in great pain or so weak that it can barely hold itself up on the perch.

Flattened plumage: If a parakeet suddenly stops what it is doing, flattens its feathers close to the body, and assumes a motionless, very upright position, it has been frightened and is petrified.

When a Bird Gets Too Warm

Raising both wings: The bird raises both wings slightly away from the body but without spreading them. This allows air to reach the underside of the wings. Some warmth is given off, and the body temperature is reduced. If it's very hot, a bird will sometimes spread both wings away from the body and pant. This also serves to lower body temperature.

Birds sometimes also raise their wings briefly when they are feeling very comfortable.

Puffing up the feathers: If a bird is sitting on its perch with puffed up feathers, it is feeling cold and trying to get warm. Air is trapped in the puffed plumage and forms an insulating layer between the body and the surrounding cold.

Yawning: All birds yawn, including parakeets. They suddenly open their bill wide and then close it again just as quickly. Yawning is as contagious among birds as it is among humans. If one bird yawns, its partner or the entire flock will soon be yawning too. Presumably parakeets yawn for the same reasons we do, namely, because they are tired or because the oxygen level in the room is low. Letting some fresh air into the room helps.

How Parakeets "Talk" to Each Other

Over the years I have learned to distinguish a number of different kinds of parakeet utterances. Watching the birds when they make these sounds has given me a good idea of when and why they are produced, and I have made up names for them. I have never come across anything like this in books and other publications on parakeets; what I am telling you here are my personal impressions.

Screeching: There are no reports of wild parakeets doing the kind of loud and often prolonged screeching that we hear many pet parakeets perform. Indeed, it seems highly unlikely to me that wild parakeets would draw attention to their nesting colony with such loud noises. According to the descriptions of naturalists, parakeets lead rather secretive lives outside the breeding season. I think that screeching is an outlet of excess energy, for living as cage birds, parakeets never have the chance to engage in enough activity.

Fear/attack sound: This sound is heard very clearly if two parakeets share a cage. It is produced whenever the dominant bird is startled or feels encroached on by its partner. The sound resembles a short cackling and is instantly understood by the bird it is addressed to. Many parakeets also produce this sound when attacking unfamiliar objects. My parakeet Clowny used to utter this sound on the bird tree, which stood on the screened-in balcony, every time he "fought" leaves rustling in the wind.

Warning call: A high-pitched, shrill, very short bird call that announces the sighting of predators. The whole flock takes to the air instantly as soon as this call is sounded.

Super-flyers

Anyone who has observed flocks of parakeets in the air is amazed at the skill and coordination the birds display. A flock changes direction without the slightest apparent difficulty, all birds acting together as though one organism. No confusion arises. This is because flocking animals, such as birds, have highly acute sensory organs with which they perceive every move and sound their neighbors make, and therefore are able to avoid collisions.

Feeding sound: A male intent on feeding his mate keeps uttering even-pitched chirping sounds. The chirping is barely audible, but the accompanying behavior is very striking. He keeps bowing to the hen and circling her with tiny steps, his pupils narrowed and his head feathers standing on end.

Begging sound: Baby parakeets and females wanting to be fed emit the typical begging sound. As they do so, they hunch down slightly and droop their wings.

Demand cry: This is very different from the begging sound. It is brief, not piercing like the warning call, and lets the other bird know that something is expected of it. Usually it means "Come here!"

Social Behavior

Since parakeets never live alone in nature but always in flocks, they have to be able to coexist as peacefully as possible. As we have seen, every bird has an inborn set of differentiated behavior patterns that regulate social life.

These behavior patterns involve voice, posture, or sequences of motions, and their meaning is immediately understood by all the members of the flock. Courtship, mating, brood care, and relations within the flock in general—including aggression—are regulated by the typical behavior patterns of the species. Many of these signaling patterns also have an effect, either soothing or exciting, on internal mood. Here are two examples:

Mutual head scratching: If you have a pair of parakeets you will have observed them taking turns scratching each other's head with obvious enjoyment. The activity has a soothing effect. No doubt, the main function of mutual head scratching is to strengthen the pair bond. It doesn't matter whether the birds are a real pair or belong to the same sex because in the latter case one of them will assume the role of the missing gender.

Mutual head scratching also serves a hygienic purpose. The small feathers on the head can be smoothed and the dust particles

The oil or preen gland is located just above the root of the long tail feathers. The birds use the gland's oily secretion to grease the entire plumage and make it water repellent. The oil also keeps the bill and the toes smooth and elastic.

A parakeet picking up the secretion from the preen gland with its bill.

The head is rubbed directly over the gland.

The undersides of the wings are constantly groomed.

removed much better by a partner than by a single bird that has to use its feet to do the job.

If at some point your parakeet presents its head to you somewhat hunched down and with the head feathers slightly raised, it is asking you to scratch it. Gently run your little finger over the bird's head against the lay of the feathers for as long as the bird holds still. But be prepared for the bird to reciprocate, starting to nibble on the hairs on your arm, your head, your cheek, or on your ear lobe.

Aggression: Basically, parakeets are peace-loving birds that flee from their enemies and don't fight over rank. Still, acts of aggression do occur in a flock. In nature, birds resort to aggressive behavior to assert their individual needs, to compete against rivals when choosing partners, and to defend their breeding sites. In most cases assumption of the typical threatening gesture is all that is necessary: tense posture with flattened down plumage, body stretched high, head turned toward the other bird.

This warning is accompanied by a threatening call. If this does not have the desired effect, the parakeet straightens its foot joints to appear even taller and reinforces its threat by hacking into the air with open beak. This is usually enough to put the opponent to flight.

As far as I know, real fights in which birds get seriously hurt occur only among birds that are kept in cages or aviaries. Females are as a rule more aggressive than males but resort to the same methods of fighting.

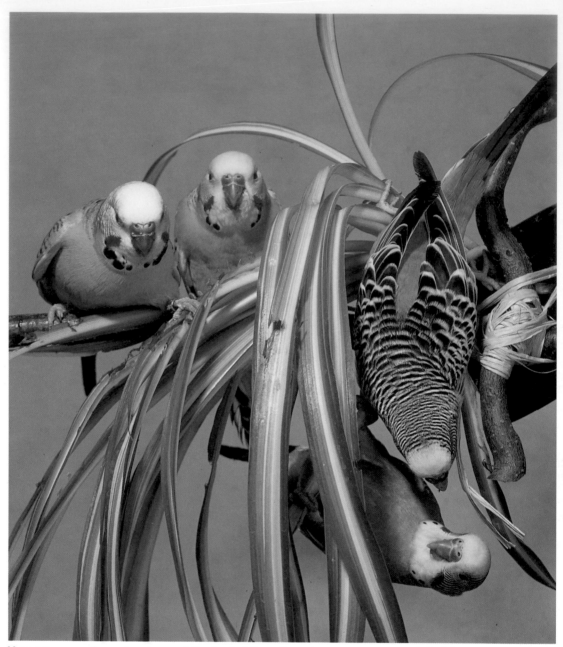

Not every aggressive gesture is meant "seriously." Sometimes these gestures are used playfully to test their effect.

Baby birds that have just left the nest have not yet developed any fear of humans. Such a "naturally tame" bird gets used to a person quickly if this person spends a lot of time with it during the first few days.

Seeing, Hearing...

As in all higher animals, the senses of sight, hearing, touch, smell, and taste are well developed in parakeets. They enable the birds to perceive their environment and to respond appropriately to what is happening around them.

Seeing: Parakeets can register 150 images per second as compared to merely 16 for humans. For these fast-flying birds instantaneous recognition of details is crucial. Because their eyes are set far to the side of the head, the birds have almost total panoramic vision. Such a large field of vision is of great advantage in spotting enemies quickly.

Scientists have shown that parakeets see the world in color, just the way we do. This makes sense because parakeets are active during the day and their plumage is brightly colored. The colors of the plumage can function as signals in the communal life only if the birds can actually see them.

Hearing: Almost all birds, including parakeets, have a highly acute sense of hearing. Parakeets can hear sounds from 400 to 20,000 Hz and are able to store sound sequences in their memory. This is important because certain calls, like the warning cry, always have to be produced spontaneously and accurately if they are to be effective. If a parakeet hears a rapid sequence of sounds, it is able to analyze it and reproduce the sequence in exact detail.

Feeling: Like many other birds, parakeets have a well developed sense of touch. Thus, a brooding hen feels with her brood patch (see Glossary) when the embryo is moving inside the egg and when the chick is getting ready to hatch. Parakeets are also sensitive to vibration. This enables them to become aware and accurately interpret even the faintest vibrations. Thus, they sense when a predator approaches the nesting or sleeping cavity, when a storm is in the making, or when a bush fire has started. In our pet birds this sense can trigger panic at night if, say, a truck rumbles by on the street or people are dancing next-door, causing vibrations whose cause the bird can't recognize. That is why the bird cage should be located where it is not subject to vibrations. Never put it on the refrigerator even for a moment, let alone on a washing machine that is in operation. In its instinctive flight reaction, the bird might seriously injure itself.

Tasting: I am convinced that parakeets have nerve cells that respond to taste, for almost every parakeet has its own food preferences. The favorite food may be a certain kind of fruit or a dish from your table that the bird always goes after, completely ignoring everything else on the table.

Smelling: I don't know whether parakeets have much of a sense of smell or not. I have never observed any of them reacting to smells. But the parakeet expert Berta Ragotzi claims that her parakeet Putzi could tell from the cooking smells what food she was preparing and would get restless when she cooked his favorite foods.

Gestures of Embarrassment

A parakeet that suddenly gets uneasy about what it is doing will engage in a displacement activity. Thus, when our playing became too rough, Manky, who loved games with a passion, would suddenly run to his food dish and start eating. If I toned the game down, he would come back to continue playing with great enthusiasm. For the first couple of months of living with me, Manky accepted me only if I was wearing one of two dresses. He was pleased whenever I entered the room and always prepared to fly up to me to greet me. If I was wearing the "wrong" dress, he would usually notice it at the last moment, stop, and start grooming himself—a typical displacement activity.

A Parakeet and Its Tail Feathers

Ordinarily a parakeet pays little attention to its tail feathers. It will often choose to sit on a perch where the tail feathers rub against something, are bent, or get scruffy. Many parakeets have tails that always look messy, but this doesn't seem to bother them. If, however, anyone—human or animal—so much as touches the tail feathers, the bird instantly shrinks away and turns around. When I had the pair Mini and Manky, I often observed Manky, in the course of his courtship display, trying to step on Mini's tail when they were both on the floor. Mini would immediately utter a cackling fear/attack cry, get away from Manky, and then direct the threat display at him. If a visitor happened to touch Manky's tail by mistake, Manky uttered the same cry and immediately tried to get away.

Justified Protest

My birds always protested when I—always for some good reason—left one or two of them in the cage while another was allowed to fly free in the room. The parakeets left behind in the cage would run back and forth along the barred wall on the cage floor like wild cats in a zoo, or they would go through such contortions that I often worried they might dislocate a leg. Hanging from the bars, they would stretch the head down between the legs, turning a complete somersault.

Amazing Feats of Parakeets

It is my opinion that parakeets are remarkably intelligent. Otto Konig, an ethologist, has demonstrated in experiments that parakeets can count (see Glossary). But quite apart from the question of counting, my birds have given surprising evidence of intelligence.

For a while, when I had the parakeet pair Manky and Mini, I was also taking care of another parakeet female, named Muschi. Muschi was a small, dainty bird, and she was determined to win Manky's affections. Mini, however, always managed to prevent the two from getting close. The chasing often ended with Muschi being bloodied. But Muschi had a way of getting back at Mini for the merci-less persecutions. When Mini was in her cage and started eating from her food dish, which hung from the bars by two hooks, Muschi would quickly climb up on the outside of the cage and push the food dish back and forth until Mini lost her appetite.

Then there was the male parakeet Zwutschi who always remained an outsider in my small flock of birds. He dared eat only when the other birds were busy flying or playing. To make sure that he was getting enough to eat, I fed him a small extra portion of hulled oats twice a day. I gave him the oats next to his little mirror on my telephone table. This was his favorite spot, and the other birds stayed away from it. Whenever I forgot the special feeding, he tried to remind me. He would pace back and forth between the mirror and the table edge, staring at me the whole time. If I failed to react, he would shove the mirror toward the table edge until it tumbled to the floor—a signal that couldn't be ignored!

Manky enjoyed a similar privilege. He got his oats in front of a small agate box on my desk that was his most favorite object in the world. While eating his oats, he would literally lie on his belly next to the box, so that Mini, sitting on her favorite perch on the bird tree, would not notice him. If Mini unexpectedly turned up on the desk during these times, she immediately pushed Manky out of the way and consumed the oats herself. Then Manky would fly directly over her head several times, uttering the demand cry, thus making her fly with him. Or if one of his little plastic balls was lying on the desk, he would throw it at her. Luckily he always missed, but he did succeed every time in driving her away from his oats.

This type of thicket of leaves offers wonderful opportunities for hiding.

If you want to understand parakeets, you have to spend a lot of time with them and, preferably, have more than one bird to observe. The birds, of course, have to have a big enough area to live in with several landing platforms where they can amuse themselves. If you have two or more birds, you can watch the forming of pairs, various forms of social interaction, and many typical behavior patterns of parakeets.

Glossary

What do terms like "French molt" and "yellow-faced" mean in the context of parakeets? This short glossary explains some general as well as a number of more specialized terms and concepts used by aviculturists. By consulting it, you can increase your understanding of these small, delightful cage birds. The words in small capital letters that appear in the text are terms alphabetically listed in this glossary.

Ability to count

Scientific experiments have shown that some animals have the ability to count and to react to numbers in specific ways. Thus, some birds learn to open food containers with a certain number of dots on them. In experiments where a bird is shown a certain number of dots and has to open a container with the same number of dots on it, it has been demonstrated that jackdaws can distinguish groups of dots numbering up to six. Parakeets and ravens perform similarly, while pigeons recognize groups of up to eight dots.

Abnormal feather growth

In older birds that are not getting an optimal diet or are not in perfect health, the feathers growing in after the MOLT may be malformed. Long tail and wing feathers as well as smaller feathers remain stuck in their sheaths with only a small tuft fanning out at the top. Feathers may also taper halfway up and turn around their axis corkscrew-fashion; they may be frayed to the tip, lose the original color, or turn dark. Likely causes are incorrect diet, hormone imbalance, or feather cysts. If you notice any such abnormal feathers, consult the vet. Only a vet can prescribe proper treatment.

Aggression

This term takes in all behavior associated with defense, attack, and threatening. Parakeet cocks threaten rivals with INTIMIDATION DISPLAYS or by pushing one foot against the adversary's breast. Hens, by contrast, attack a rival without noticeable warning signs and immediately start biting. Females are more aggressive than males. If you have a parakeet pair you don't have to worry about fights because the cock never attacks his mate, and he almost always lets her eat first.

Alarm call

A special, shrill call, which parakeets utter to warn the flock against danger. As soon as they hear this call, the birds rise quickly up into the air. You can sometimes observe this in pet parakeets if a bird catches sight of a raptor through a window or is frightened by something else.

Albinos

White parakeets without any markings. These birds lack MELANIN and belong to the blue series. Albinos have red eyes and a pink CERE.

Aspergillosis

A fungus infection of the air passages, usually caused by dry or wet moldy food, hay, straw, and similar items. It is caught by breathing in the spores of the fungus *Aspergillus fumigatus*. The spores germinate in the lungs and air sacs producing toxic substances that damage the tissues lining the respiratory system. See your veterinarian immediately.

Automatic food dispensers

Usually tube-shaped plastic containers that are filled with birdseed. The seeds automatically slide down into a small trough, where the parakeets can get at them. The advantage of dispensers is that the birds always have clean food available, but it is important to check every day to make sure the feeder is working properly and the seeds don't get stuck in the tube. Many a parakeet has starved to death with a hopper full of food in front of it but no seeds in the trough because they were blocked in the tube.

Billing and cooing

Sounds made by a pair of parakeets that have taken a liking to each other. They often sit close together, preen each other, and bill and coo. In order to stimulate the hen's mating urge, the cock repeatedly taps his bill against hers. During courtship feeding, the bills of the two birds are hooked together at right angles, and the male regurgitates food from his crop.

Brood patch

Developed on the abdomen by brooding females during the incubating period. In these places the skin thickens and receives more blood flow, thus delivering more warmth for the eggs. Through these brood patches, the mother bird can also feel movement within the eggs and is thus aware when a chick is getting ready to hatch. In many bird species the brood patches become completely bare; in parakeets the plumage just gets thinner.

Brooding

The mother bird keeps her nestlings warm, or "broods" them, by sitting on the nest with slightly extended wings, underneath which the chicks huddle close to the mother's body.

Buffs

Buff parakeets (which are of greater size than average birds) are pale yellow with buff as the ground color. The head spots (and the head itself) are much greater in size than normal. The large "buff" flight and tail feathers are broad and long, and the yellow does not extend to the edges, which has the effect of dulling the color.

Carotenoid

The yellow, orange, and red colors that are responsible, together with MELANIN, for the colors (in feathers, eyes, feet, nails, and beak) of a parakeet. The colors don't show up until the feather tissue turns horny. Then they appear first in diffused form along the barbs and barblets as these turn keratinous. The pigment is deposited in dissolved form directly in the keratinous tissue that is forming.

Cere

Located at the base of the upper mandible and surrounding the nostrils. In parakeets, the cere is bare of feathers. The cere of immature parakeets of both sexes is light pink or light beige. After the first molt it turns a vivid blue in males. In the hen it remains light beige or becomes brownish. In some strains, as in the HARLEQUINS, this difference between the sexes no longer exists, and the cere of the adult male, too, is light beige.

Chromosomes

Microscopic, thread-like structures within the cell nucleus that carry the hereditary information (see MENDEL'S LAW) of an organism in the form of genes, which are located on them in pairs.

Cinnamons

Parakeets with brown barring. The color is produced by a brown pigment (see MELANIN). The throat spots and large feathers are also brown.

Clearwings

Parakeets whose markings are faded to a light gray because of a dilution of the MELANIN. The wings and tail feathers are also gray or, more rarely, yellow.

Colony breeders

All birds that breed in groups in nature. Some birds breed in dense proximity, nest next to nest. Others breed in looser colonies, with the nests separated by several feet. Parakeets are among this latter group. They

Glossary

are peaceful flock birds that, if they have enough room to get out of each other's way, fight only rarely. In captivity, several pairs can therefore be placed in an aviary to breed.

Color breeding
The original color of parakeets is light green with a yellow face and the typical wavy lines on the back of the head, back, and wing coverts (see ORIGINAL STRAIN). All other color types were created by breeders.

Communication of mood
Like many other kinds of animals that live in social groups, parakeets communicate their moods to each other. If, for example, a group of parakeets has been foraging on the ground for some time and one bird takes off because it is no longer hungry, the others soon follow suit and the entire flock takes to the air. Or, if one bird preens itself, its neighbors will do the same. Thanks to this mechanism, a group of birds is able to keep all its members together, thus providing protection against dangers to individual birds.

Copulation
Mating. When parakeets get ready to mate, the male climbs onto the female's back with both feet. The female's tail feathers are raised, so that the two birds' vents touch and the semen can penetrate to the hen's oviduct.

Courtship display
This term is used to include all behavior patterns leading up to COPULATION, from mate selection to the formation and strengthening of the pair bond.

Crested parakeets
Crested parakeets come in all combinations of colors and markings. There are three types of crests: The full-circular crest, which is made up of a tuft of longer feathers on the center of the head. The feathers form a fringe all around the head that comes down in the front almost to the eyes, somewhat like bangs. The eyes are not covered. The second type is the half-circular, which is like the full-circular but limited to the front of the head. The third type is the tufted, in which the crest consists only of some feathers on the forehead that stick up straight.

Dimorphism
See SEXUAL DIMORPHISM.

Disinfecting
The cage and other places where the parakeets spend time, as well as food dishes, perches, and objects the birds play with have to be disinfected regularly and then hosed clean with warm water and rubbed dry. This helps prevent disease. Only mild disinfectants that contain no formaldehyde should be used. Formaldehyde is highly toxic and bad for the birds' health. If you're not sure what product to use, ask your vet. He or she can

also prescribe disinfectants effective against specific pathogens. Always read the manufacturer's instructions before use.

Displacement activity
Common in situations where a bird is torn between two conflicting impulses, for instance, fight and flight. If neither impulse wins out over the other, the bird will often resort to a so-called displacement activity. That is, it engages in an activity that seems completely irrelevant, such as scratching, grooming, or eating.

Domestication
The process, going on over many generations, during which a wild animal is gradually transformed into a domestic animal or a pet. Parakeets became domesticated by being bred for many decades in captivity, where natural selection plays no role and man decides which individuals will reproduce.

Double buffs
Parakeets with even longer and broader feathers and thus an even duller color than regular buffs. Double buffs result from the mating of two buffs.

Egg binding
Term used to describe a hen's difficulty in laying eggs and especially the inability of pressing the egg out of the oviduct and expelling it out of the vent. The lower belly looks rounded, and the hen grows increasingly

weak as she strains with raised feathers and closed eyes. If exposure to an infrared heat lamp produces no results after one or two hours, the bird has to be taken to the vet as quickly as possible.

Egg laying
Parakeet hens lay eggs every other day until there is a clutch of three to five or, rarely, more eggs. The egg is expelled through the strong pressure exerted by the muscles surrounding the oviduct. After the egg is laid, the hen remains motionless for about five minutes to recover from the effort. If a hen suffers from EGG BINDING, the vet has to be called immediately. Apparently the reproductive urge is often so strong in parakeet hens that they skip the preliminary stages of courtship, pair formation, and mating and produce eggs even when alone or with only a second female as companion. These hens gradually exhaust their physical reserves and can die of weakness if no hormone treatments are used to stop them from laying.

Egg tooth
A hard, calcareous, thorn-shaped protuberance on the upper mandible of a chick. With this egg tooth, the chick is able to pip the shell, which it then breaks open with stretching movements. The egg tooth is shed five to seven days after hatching.

Euthanasia
The act of mercifully putting a living being to death. An animal should be killed only by a veterinarian and only if its life constitutes a threat to others or if it suffers inordinately without hope of recovery. If a parakeet is incurably sick, it should be put to sleep by the vet with an injection.

Excreta
Waste matter. Parakeets produce small droppings every 12 to 15 minutes. The droppings of a healthy bird consist of a small, dark green to black ring surrounding a core of whitish, semi-solid urine. Preceding and during egg laying, females tend to produce softer droppings, and while incubating, they deposit clearly larger droppings at longer intervals.

F allows
Parakeets with reddish brown markings and red eyes. European continental fallows have a white iris; the British strains have no visible iris ring.

Feather cysts
Caused by quills that fail to break through the skin. If they are not taken care of in time, a bulge-like swelling can develop. Cysts should be cut open and treated only by a vet.

Featherduster
Parakeets whose feathers keep growing and eventually interfere with flying as well as with see-ing. It is still unclear whether this condition is an inherited MUTATION or an abnormal condition. Most featherdusters are very aggressive. Many also have difficulties eating and eventually starve to death. Because they are also very susceptible to infections, featherdusters usually don't live long.

Feather mites
See PARASITES.

Feather plucking
Large parrots kept singly often start plucking their feathers and sometimes keep at it until they are completely naked except for the head. This is relatively rare in parakeets. It is still unclear at this point whether this "bad habit" is psychological in nature or is caused by incorrect feeding, metabolic imbalances, or parasites. Many reports of this serious condition indicate that parrots, as well as parakeets, first started to pluck feathers when they were separated from the person they were attached to or from their avian partner. But there are also cases where a single bird lived for years in human company and then suddenly and without apparent reason began to pluck itself. Whatever the final word may be, you should always take a feather-plucking bird to the vet to get his or her advice. Paying more attention to the bird and getting it a companion of its own species may bring about an improvement. Sometimes the hen starts to pluck out the feathers of her

Glossary

chicks. There are various liquids available to spray onto the chicks, which should deter the female parent. If nothing stops her from feather plucking, she should be removed and the cock left to rear the youngsters.

Feet of parakeets
Parakeets have the typical climbing feet of parrots with the two middle toes pointing forward and the two outer ones, backward. This kind of foot is beautifully adapted for holding onto branches and can also be used for holding food. Although parakeets don't raise food to their bill with the foot the way larger parrots do, they do sometimes grasp a millet spray with the foot and pull it closer in order to pick out the small grains more easily.

Flock
A flock of parakeets forms a loose breeding colony and, outside of the breeding season, lives in regions that provide sufficient food and water. When the food begins to get scarce, the flock takes off in search of new feeding grounds, ranging hundreds of miles across the continent. On these journeys many flocks come together and form super flocks of several hundred or thousand birds.

Foster rearing
If an egg or a young chick is added to the nest of an unrelated pair, which then brood and rear it along with their own offspring, it is called foster rearing.

French molt
A disease, often called Budgerigar Beak and Feather Disease, characterized by incomplete development of the feathers limited to parakeets and several small Australian parakeets (for example turquoisine, Bourke, and splendid mutations). It can affect nestlings as young as four weeks old. The large wing and tail feathers that have just grown in fall out or break off and are then either not replaced at all or fall out again before the birds can fly. As a rule, these birds never learn to fly and are often called "runners" or "creepers." They can develop into very tame pets in spite of this, though they require a lot of care. They should be kept in a large cage where they have plenty of opportunity for climbing and gnawing. Parakeets with French molt should never be bred or combined with healthy breeding pairs because it is suspected that the disease may be transmitted by a virus. In some cases runners do recover and grow normal feathers. After the first MOLT it is impossible to tell that these birds were previously runners.

Full-circular crested
See CRESTED.

G enetics
See MENDEL'S LAW.

Genus
A category in the classification of organisms. A genus generally includes several closely related SPECIES. The next higher category is the family. The first word in the Latin name of a plant or animal (see NOMENCLATURE) is always capitalized and stands for the genus.

Geographical subspecies
Evolve in habitats with climatic differences. The two SUBSPECIES of *Melopsittacus undulatus* are geographical subspecies. The climate of northern Australia is hotter than that of western Australia, and the parakeets in the two regions developed small differences in color and markings from the original STRAIN.

Ghost markings
The very faint markings of a parakeet whose gentic make-up is deficient in MELANIN. Ghost markings do not turn up accidentally but are deliberately created by breeders.

Growth of bill
The upper mandible, or maxilla, of a parakeet has a movable joint by which it is connected to the head bone. The lower mandible has a sliding joint that allows the jaw to move back and forth horizontally. Thus the bill is highly mobile. If CAROTENOID birds are kept properly, the horny substance of the bill (keratin) is continually worn down through gnawing on branches, the cuttlebone, and the mineral block. This natural wear is balanced by the continual growth of the bill. In older parakeets, the bill can grow at an abnormal rate

because of hormonal and metabolic imbalances, so that the bill no longer works properly. The tip of the maxilla may curl all the way over the lower mandible, or the lower mandible may grow sideways. In either case the bird will sooner or later be unable to eat. Take the bird to the vet to have the bill cut to proper shape and to correct as much as possible the condition that is causing the abnormality.

Half-circular crested
See CRESTED PARAKEETS.

Half-siders
Parakeets that are a combination of two different color types due to a partial loss of the genetic inheritance during cell division (see Introduction to Genetics, page 105). Such a bird may thus, for example, be half green and half blue. This change in appearance cannot be passed on to future generations.

Harlequins
Birds with pied plumage, also called recessive (Danish) PIEDS. The name "harlequin" arose because the patches of different colors are reminiscent of the many-colored costume of the commedia dell'arte character Harlequin.

Head scratching
Birds can be assigned to two groups on the basis of how they scratch their heads. One group raises the foot up directly to the head for scratching; the other

raises the foot under the wing or from behind the wing to reach to the head. Parakeets belong to this second group.

Homeopathy
The treatment of disease using very small amounts of a medication that would in healthy organisms produce symptoms of the disease treated.
Homeopathic medicine is effective against many ailments. Always ask the vet about homeopathic treatments because these generally have no harmful side effects.

Homing instinct
We know that many migratory birds return every year to the breeding grounds they left in the previous fall. This is called the homing instinct. These birds are able to orient themselves by certain features of the landscape or by the position of the stars. Parakeets, by contrast, are nomads. They have no need for a homing instinct, but they do, of course, learn their way around in whatever breeding ground they occupy, and they have no trouble finding their breeding site again even after far-ranging flights to find water. By contrast, a cage bird that escapes finds itself in a completely unfamiliar world and has no chance of finding its way home again.

Hybrids
Offspring of individuals belonging to two different SPECIES. Unless the two species are closely related or are actually sub-

species of the same species, no offspring will result from matings. In the overwhelming majority of cases hybrids cannot reproduce.

Inbreeding
Breeding pure strains cannot be accomplished without inbreeding. If trails that differ from the norm are to be established, the breeder has to resort to mating parents with offspring, mating of siblings, and mating of more distantly related birds. Decreasing fertility and declining resistance are the negative side effects of inbreeding.

Incubation temperature
The ideal incubation temperature for parakeets is 99°F (37°C). If the room temperature is between 61 to 64°F (16–18°C), the close contact with the mother's body creates an environment of about 99°F (37°C) for the eggs. If the room is cooler, the hatching date—eggs hatch after incubating for an average of 18 days—may be delayed.

Individual recognition
Individual recognition is the ability not only to tell whether other birds belong to the same species but also to recognize individual birds in the flock and, especially, the bird's own mate and offspring. Individual recognition is a precondition for any kind of social bonds to develop. Recognition may be based on sound utterances or external characteristics.

Glossary

Ino factor

The ino factor has the effect of masking all the genes of the green series parakeets to produce the LUTINO, and all the genes of the blue series parakeets, except one, to produce the ALBINO. The one gene in the blue series that the ino factor seems incapable of masking is the YELLOW FACE. When these two genes are present in one bird, a yellow-faced albino is the result. Although the ino factor appears to be dominant to all colors, it does not affect varieties. Crested albinos and lutinos are quite common.

Intelligence

See ABILITY TO COUNT.

Intimidation display

Term used by ethologists to describe behavior that serves to impress other members of the species. Parakeets have a number of stereotypical behavior patterns that are used to impress or intimidate. One of them is the slight raising of the feathers on the forehead accompanied by a stretching of the body and a stiff-legged pacing with tiny steps. Loud knocking of the bill against wood is also meant to impress. Which form of display behavior is used depends on whether a bird wants to scare off a rival or woo a female.

Juvenile

Not yet sexually mature.

Lacewings

The result of crossing CINNAMONS with INOS. They are white or yellow with pale brownish markings (ghost markings), have red eyes, and are SEX-LINKED.

Life expectancy

Expected length of time an organism will live. Given proper care and loving attention, pet parakeets can live to an average of 12 to 14 years.

Lutino

A yellow parakeet of the green series without markings and with red eyes. The yellow color is caused by the pigment psittacine. Lutinos have a pink CERE and white cheek spots.

Melanin

Dark pigment. Two groups of pigments are responsible for the colors (in feathers, eyes, feet, nails, and beak) of parakeets: MELANIN and CAROTENOID. Melanin is the dark pigment (black, gray, and brown) of the feathers, eyes, beak, feet, and nails. The color of human hair mainly is due to melanin. The black or dark brown melanins that don't dissolve readily are called eumelanins, the dark red to yellow, easily soluble ones, pheomelanins. Eumelanin accounts for the brown markings in cinnamons, for example, while pheomelanin causes the reddish brown in FALLOWS.

Mendel's Law

The principle of inheritance first formulated in the nineteenth century by Gregor Johann Mendel, an Augustinian prior and teacher of natural science. In experiments crossing different strains of green peas, Mendel discovered the basic law that dominates the inheritance of simple traits. If the two genes responsible for an alternate characteristic (such as tall or dwarf growth of pea plants) are different, only one of them can dominate; that is, only one form shows up in the offspring. The other gene is recessive; that is, the alternate characteristic seems to disappear. However, it is still present in the genetic make-up of the individual and can show up again in future generations. It was not until the early twentieth century that other scientists confirmed the truth of Mendel's discovery and demonstrated the universal application of his law in the reproduction of all organisms.

Molt

A natural process that serves to renew the plumage. Parakeets lose a lot of feathers during the molt, but their appearance is only temporarily affected when the large feathers fall out. The small contour feathers grow back within a few days, but the large ones take several weeks. Parakeets living wild in Australia molt at irregular intervals, usually toward the end of a breeding cycle and before the entire flock leaves the breeding grounds.

Cage parakeets generally molt once a year. If there are major and frequent temperature fluctuations, there are often several minor molts in between. Young birds undergo a fairly radical "baby" molt from which they emerge with adult plumage. After that, the molts are partial. The younger and healthier a bird, the less the molt will affect its overall state. Older and weak parakeets sometimes look sick while they molt. Molting only rarely prevents parakeets from flying. If you notice that one of your birds has difficulties landing or taking off, provide some assistance in the form of hemp ropes or branches that make it easier to climb to the sleeping or sitting perch and to the cage entrance.

Molt caused by fright
If a bird is frightened because it has been grasped awkwardly, it may lose whole bunches of feathers. This behavior evolved in many kinds of wild birds as a defense against predators that grasp their prey. Although parakeets usually recover from the fright, the feathers may take several weeks to grow back.

Monogamy
Having only one mate. Like most parrots, parakeets are monogamous. In nature, the partner, of course, belongs to the opposite sex since the purpose of these permanent bonds is instant readiness to breed when conditions are favorable.

Mutation
A change in the hereditary material that can be passed on to the offspring.

Newcastle Disease (Velogenic Viscerotropic Newcastel Disease or VVND)
A much feared virus infection that affects birds and especially domestic fowl. The disease can be transmitted from birds to humans. After a brief illness, lasting usually only six to nine days, almost all the birds die. The symptoms are: diarrhea, discharge from nostrils and eyes, paralysis, twisting the neck, breathing difficulty. The disease is highly contagious, and a conclusive diagnosis is possible only if the autopsy of dead birds reveals the virus in the organs. Because the disease is so contagious and deadly, any incidence has to be reported. The veterinarian will initiate the necessary procedures.

Nomenclature
A system of terms used in biology to name animals and plants according to specific rules. In the mid-1700s the Swedish physician and natural scientist Carolus Linnaeus introduced binary nomenclature to classify all the organisms he knew. In this system each plant and animal species is given a name consisting of two parts. The first word, always capitalized, stands for the genus; the second, written lower-case, indicates the species. Since the beginning of this century, subspecies are indicated by adding a third word, which is also written lower-case.

Nominate form
See ORIGINAL STRAIN.

Opalines
Parakeets in which the barring and the wing markings are much reduced. The fine lines of the barring typical of parakeets are, in opalines, more widely spaced and less well defined on the head, neck, and back. The nape and back exhibit the bird's ground color, and the clear area on the back is bordered by the the dark markings on the wings to form a "V" shape. The markings on the back are in the bird's ground color (green, blue, or gray), not rimmed with yellow or white as in other parakeets. This creates an opalescent effect, which is reflected in the name of the birds.

Original strain
The original strain of cage-bred parakeets is light green. These birds have the coloration and markings of a wild parakeet: a yellow mask and six round, black dots on the throat, the outermost ones covered up by the longish, violet cheek spots. The ground color of the underside and the rump is light green, and the undulating lines on head, cheeks, neck, back, and wings are black. The long tail feathers are dark blue; the legs and feet are bluish gray.

Glossary

Ornithology
The scientific study of birds.

Ornithosis
See PSITTACOSIS.

Parasites

An organism that lives in or off another organism. Both internal and external parasites can give rise to diseases. Among external parasites found on parakeets are the following:

Red bird mite: This pest lives on the blood of its host. Hiding in cracks in the cage and perches during the day, it attacks the birds at night. If the mites become very numerous, they stay on the birds during the day, hiding under the wings. They show up under a strong magnifying glass as tiny dots, red or blackish depending on whether they have just absorbed blood or have already digested it. If the birds are breeding, the mites stay in the nesting box during the day, and even a minor infestation can lead to the death of nestlings because of the constant loss of blood. Infested birds keep pecking at their feathers nervously and scratching. They should be taken to the vet for treatment. The vet will also recommend a disinfectant that is effective against these mites and should be used on the cage, the perch outside, and all objects the bird comes in contact with. Red mites can also move to other pets and to humans.

Cnemidocoptes pilae: This mite causes scaly face. The condition manifests itself in light gray to whitish encrustations, riddled with tiny burrowing holes, near the eyelids, on the beak, and sometimes on the CERE and the legs as well. The mites make small pockets in the epidermis that, in advanced cases, honeycomb the entire skin. As a rule younger birds are afflicted with scaly face. An outbreak of the disease can be brought on by stress, poor environmental conditions, or by weakened resistance. The parasite may be present in passive form in parakeets for a number of years without the disease flaring up. The affected parts of the body should be treated with drugs recommended by the vet.

Feather mites: These wingless insects feed on skin and feather particles and cause severe itching. The mites crawling around on the skin make the birds very nervous. Partially gnawed feathers are a visible sign of this pest. Feather mites, too, should be treated with drugs recommended by the vet.

Parental care

Includes all activities directed toward the production, maintenance, and support of offspring. It starts with those patterns of behavior that indicate the desire to mate and produce offspring. This behavior is triggered by certain environmental stimuli that differ from species to species. For many songbirds, increasing daylight is the decisive factor. In parakeets the reproductive urge awakens when there are rainfalls that promise sufficient availability of water and the sprouting of fresh grass. Since pet parakeets are abundantly supplied with both water and food, they enter the reproductive mood with relative frequency. In this mood they start trying to feed regurgitated food to their mirror image, a plastic bird, or some other object. In males this is a surrogate action for feeding the mate, in females, for feeding chicks.

Pheomelanin
See MELANIN.

Pied parakeets
Parakeets with areas of different colors. There are Continental dominant, Danish recessive, and Australian dominant pieds. The Danish recessive pieds are also called HARLEQUINS. Pieds occur in the varous shades of the blue and the green series (see Genetics) and usually have light patches on the nape and lightened color on the long wing and tail feathers.

Plumage
The plumage of a bird is made up of a great many soft and flexible but extremely durable feathers. There are several kinds of feathers, which differ from each other in form and function. The most obvious are the contour feathers. They cover the bird's body and keep it from getting wet. The long wing and tail feathers enable the bird to fly. Because of their complex structure they can function in various ways. The down feathers

hidden underneath the contour feathers serve primarily as insulation to keep the birds warm. Parakeet chicks, which remain in the nest and are fed by their parents until they are ready to fly, usually have only down feathers for the first few days before the contour feathers begin to grow in.

Poisonous plants

Plants can spell danger for parakeets. The following house plants are highly poisonous for parakeets and should therefore not be kept anywhere near birds: Amaryllis, azalea, balsam pear, caladium, chalice vine, false henbane, deadly amanita, death camas, delphinium, jack-in-the-pulpit, primula, lobelia, locoweed, mayapple, snowdrop, snow-on-the-mountain (ghost weed), *Strychos nux vomica*, catharanthus, holly, all Dieffenbachia species, yew, hyacinth, periwinkle (*Vinca minor*), all plants of the nightshade family (*Solanum spp*), Pachypodium, narcissi, oleander, berries of *Ardisia*, poinsettia, *Cordiaeum variegatum*, Indian licorice (Rosary pea), and berries of the ornamental asparagus fern. The following plants are not poisonous but irritate the mucous membranes and can be very harmful for as small a creature as a parakeet: ivy, *Monstera deliciosa*, flamingo flower, golden trumpet, *Alaonema*, philodendron, and Schefflera. Caution is also in order with cacti and other plants with spiny parts. Birds can injure their eyes on spines or thorns. When you buy new plants, ask if they pose any risk to birds.

Psittacosis or ornithosis

An infectious disease that occurs in songbirds, pigeons, domestic fowl, and parrots. A parakeet that has psittacosis may show any or all of the following symptoms: lethargy, sleepiness, lack of appetite, watery droppings, discharge from the nostrils, breathing difficulty, conjunctivitis with slimy secretions on the lower eyelids, and bouts of shivering. If you notice these symptoms in a bird, isolate it immediately and take it to the vet within 10 hours. Only if action is taken very promptly is there a chance of recovery.

People, too, can get psittacosis, which, in humans, is especially dangerous for older individuals and those with circulatory problems. In humans the disease resembles the flu or a mild case of pneumonia. If you have such symptoms, see your doctor and mention that you keep birds. Both birds and humans get the disease primarily from inhaling contaminated dust. During the acute stage of the disease, the birds eliminate the pathogen in their droppings, which, when dried, are swept up into the air by the bird's flapping and flying.

Even a healthy bird can be the carrier of the disease. A deterioration in the bird's overall condition, the result, perhaps, of stress, mourning, a difficult molt, or a cold, may trigger an outbreak of the disease. As a precautionary measure you may want to have a sample dropping analyzed for the presence of the pathogen.

Any occurrence of psittacosis has to be reported. The vet will tell you what you have to do. Since all pet dealers and bird breeders have to maintain records, the source of the infection can be traced back.

R ed bird mite

See PARASITES.

S caly face

See PARASITES.

Sexual dimorphism

Obvious external dissimilarities between the sexes. Thus, in wild-colored parakeets the CERE of the male is blue while that of the female is light beige.

Sleeping place

Outside the breeding period every flock of wild parakeets has its sleeping trees, where all the members of the flock gather shortly before nightfall. Our caged parakeets, too, need a special place for sleeping. This can be a branch inside the cage, the swing, or simply a corner of the cage. Always make sure the bird has time to settle in this place before turning off the light. For bird rooms or aviaries, using a dimmer switch has proven useful.

Glossary

Sleeping posture
The way in which a parakeet sleeps. Normally a sleeping parakeet rests on one leg with the foot of the other leg pulled up into the abdominal feathers. The bill is tucked in the back feathers when the bird rests or sleeps. But there are exceptions: Some parakeets sleep standing on both legs, and an occasional bird even sleeps hanging upside down, holding on with one or both feet to a bar of the cage roof.

Spangles
The markings of spangles—dark rims around white feathers on the back and wings—are the reverse of those of wild-colored parakeets, whose dark feathers on back and wings have yellow edges.

Species
A group of organisms that have the same physical structure. Some external traits can vary within a species and, in the case of extreme deviations, give rise to SUBSPECIES. For a long time it was thought that all Australian parakeets were identical. In recent years, however, Australian ornithologists (see ORNITHOLOGY) have suggested that there may be different subspecies.

Standard
The breeding ideal as defined by a cage bird society. The standard includes precise descriptions of posture, plumage, colors, and markings.

Structure of a feather
All parts of a feather consist of feather cells, whose arrangement determines the appearance and function of that particular feather. Every feather has a quill lodged in the skin and is supplied with blood and nutrients while it forms. The distal part of the quill, called the rachis, forms the flexible central shaft of the feather, from which the vanes extend on both sides. The vanes are made up of fine, stiff rays, known as barbs, and each barb has even finer rays, or barbules, growing from it. On these barbules are tiny hooks, called hamuli. Since the barbs grow at an angle of almost 45 degrees from the shaft, and the angle between the barbs and the barbules is about the same, an interlacing network is formed that is lightly held in place by the hamuli. If a vane is split for some reason, the bird merely has to shake its plumage for the hamuli to hook up again to restore the proper shape of the feather.

Subspecies
Very closely related groups of birds or other organisms that belong to the same SPECIES but differ from each other in minor, more or less obvious external characteristics. If the habitats of two subspecies overlap or if birds belonging to subspecies of the same species meet in their extensive flights, individuals of different subspecies may mate and produce so-called HYBRIDS.

Symbiosis
The living together for mutual benefit of organisms belonging to different species. It is generally assumed that some Australian *Psephotus* parakeets, for example, live in symbiosis with the larvae of small moths, which keep the birds' nests clean. However, this has actually been observed only in the case of the orange-fronted parakeet.

Topography
The type of anatomical description of an organism that explains which body parts are where and what their technical names are.

Trimming claws
Very young parakeets often have extremely sharp claws because they are not yet worn down. These birds therefore get their claws caught easily in things like cloth and can injure themselves. Don't trim the claws of these young birds with scissors; round the pointed ends with a fingernail file. Older birds sometimes have claws that have grown too long, and this, too, is dangerous. Ask the vet to do the necessary trimming because cutting into blood vessels of the claw can endanger the bird's life and must be avoided.

Tufted parakeets
See CRESTED.

U ropygial gland

Also called oil or preen gland, it is located just above the base of the tail feathers and secretes a fatty substance that helps keep the plumage waterproof and the bill, scales, and toes elastic and smooth. Parakeets run the head over the gland repeatedly and also pick up the secretion with the bill to distribute it over the plumage.

V ent

The anus of a bird. The vent, which is the external opening of the cloaca, serves not only for the elimination of excreta and urine but also for egg laying and the transfer of male semen to the female's oviduct.

W hite black-eye

A white parakeet that has all the characteristics of an ALBINO except for the eyes, which are black.

Wintering over

If your parakeets live in an outdoor aviary, they have to have access to a heatable shelter, to which they can retreat on cold nights and days. The temperature in the shelter should be about 50°F (10°C). Wild parakeets live in the hot regions of Australia and quickly move to warmer areas when it gets cold. Parakeets do survive short periods below freezing, for even in the tropical parts of Australia the temperature drops below freezing for a few hours in the night maybe ten times a year. But if they can, these small nomads avoid cold spells by moving. If aviary birds are forced to spend long winters outdoors they generally survive, but in a state that is more vegetative than truly alive.

Y ellow black-eyes

Yellow parakeets without markings except for the white cheek mark characteristic of LUTINOS. Unlike real lutinos, these birds have black eyes.

Yellow-faced

Although yellow-faced parakeets belong to the blue series, they have a yellow mask and yellow bands on the outer tail feathers. The yellow-faced trait can occur in all shades of the blue series. Yellow-faced birds occur in two mutant forms (see MUTATION): Mutant I is as described above; mutant II has, in addition, a general overlay of yellow, which makes a blue bird, for example, look greenish.

Index

Index

Useful Associations

Parakeet owners interested in exchanging information with other bird fanciers and in keeping abreast of current developments in the care and breeding of parakeets should join a national parakeet or bird society.

American Budgerigar Society
1704 Kangaroo
Killeen, TX 76543
(817) 699-3965

American Federation of Aviculture
3118 West Thomas Road
Suite 713
Phoenix, AZ 85017
(602) 484-0931

Avicultural Society of America
c/o Joe Krader
17347 Aspenglow
Yorba Linda, CA 92686
(714) 996-5538

Bird Association of California
c/o Ferdinand R. Wagner
679 Prospect
Pasadena, CA 91103
(818) 795-6621

The Budgerigar Society
(England)
57, Stephyn's Chambers
Bank Cour
Marlowes, Hemel Hempstead,
Herts

Budgerigar World (England)
County Press Buildings
Bala, North Wales, LL23 7PG

COM-U.S.A.
PO Box 122
Elizabeth, NJ 07207
(201) 353-0669

The Golden Triangle Parrot Club
PO Box 1574, Station C
Kitchener, Ontario
Canada N2G 4P4

Useful Books

For further reading on this subject, consult the following books also published by Barron's Educational Series (see address on next page).
Helen Piers: *How to Take Care of Your Parakeet*. Barron's, NY, 1993.
Annette Wolter: *Parakeets, a Complete Pet Owner's Manual*. Barron's, NY, 1990.
I. Birmelin, A. Wolter: *The New Parakeet Handbook*. Barron's, NY, 1986.
B. Moizer, S. Moizer: *The Complete Book of Budgerigars*. Barron's, NY, 1988.

Useful Magazines

The AFA Watchbird
American Federation of Aviculture
3118 West Thomas Road
Suite 713
Phoenix, AZ 85017

American Cage Bird Magazine
One Glamore Court
Smithtown, NY 11787

Bird Talk
PO Box 57347
Boulder, CO 80323

Birds USA
PO Box 55811
Boulder, CO 80322

Budgerigar World (England)
County Press Buildings
Bala, North Wales, LL23 7PG

Cage and Aviary Birds (England)
Prospect House
9-15 Ewell Road
Cheam, Sutton, Surrey SM3 8B2

Photo Credits

Ardea/Beste: Page 16; Arendt and Schweiger: Pages 11, 14/15, 142/143; Wegler: All other photos.

Acknowledgments

The author and the publisher wish to thank all the parakeet owners who contributed valuable suggestions for this book in their many readers' responses.

Special thanks are due to Herbert Hummel for checking the chapters on parakeet offspring and parakeet breeding and for his help in photographing the different color varieties; also to Klaus Stark and Karin Bladel, who assisted us in the preparation of the chapter on bird diseases and the glossary; and, finally, Karl Clemens, chairman of the Munich chapter of the Association for the Protection of Endangered Species, Bird Maintenance and Breeding Section, and Georg Helm for advice and help in photographing nestling parakeets.

Warning

This book deals with the care and maintaining of parakeets. People who are allergic to feathers or feather dust should not keep birds. If you are not sure whether you might have such an allergy, consult a doctor before buying birds.

When birds are handled, they sometimes bite or scratch. Have such wounds immediately treated by a physician.

At this time, psittacosis is very rare in parakeets (see Glossary), but if it occurs it is extremely dangerous both in birds and humans. If you have any reason to suspect psittacosis, take your bird to the veterinarian for examination, and if you have flu or cold symptoms, consult your doctor and mention that you keep birds.

© Copyright 1992 by Gräfe und Unzer GmbH, Munich. The title of the German book is *Liebenswerte Wellensittiche*. Translated from the German by Robert and Rita Kimber.

First English language edition published in 1994 by Barron's Educational Series, Inc. English translation © Copyright 1993 by Barron's Educational Series, Inc.

Address all inquiries to:
Barron's Educational Series, Inc.
250 Wireless Boulevard
Hauppauge, New York 11788.

Library of Congress Catalog Card No. 93-11625

International Standard Book No. 0-8120-1688-2

Library of Congress Cataloging-in-Publication Data

Wolter, Annette.
  [Liebenswerte Wellensittiche. English]
  The complete book of parakeet care : expert advice on proper management, 160 fascinating color photos, tips on parakeet care for children / Annette Wolter, Monika Wegler.
     p.   cm.
  Includes bibliographical references (p.   ) and index.
  Summary: Explains how to select, feed, care for, and breed parakeets.
  ISBN 0-8120-1688-2
  1. Budgerigar. [1. Parakeets. 2. Pets.]   I. Wegler, Monika.
  II. Title.
SF473.B8W6313   1994   93-11625
636.6 ' 864—dc20   CIP
                                                            AC

PRINTED IN HONG KONG

4567   987654321

Seeing a picture like this of a flock of parakeets always reminds us that parakeets have to be free to fly.

Only if they can fly can they live a full life as birds.

Fallow dark blue (cock).

Clearwing opaline dark blue (hen).

Clearwing olive green (cock).

Green–Blue–White...

The photo on the right shows a clearwing opaline dark blue cock (on left) and a rainbow cock (on right).

Two particularly lovely color varieties.